EXTENDING SCIENCE 2

WATER
Selected Topics
Second Edition

BROWNEDGE ST. MARY'S
R.C. HIGH SCHOOL
STATION ROAD,
BAMBER BRIDGE, PRESTON.
PRESTON 39813

Extending Science Series

1	Air	E N Ramsden and R E Lee
2	Water	E N Ramsden and R E Lee
3	Diseases and Disorders	P T Bunyan
4	Sounds	J J Wellington
5	Metals and Alloys	E N Ramsden
6	Land and Soil	R E Lee
7	Energy	J J Wellington
8	Life Worldwide	T Carrick
9	Nuclear Power	R E Lee
10	Forensic Science	T H James
11	Biotechnology	J Teasdale
12	Pregnancy and Birth	S D Tunnicliffe
13	Sport	R B Arnold
14	Cells, Cancers and Communities	A Charlton
15	Food	E N Ramsden
16	The Chemical Industry	R E Lee
17	Astronomy	B Abrams and P Moore

Further titles are being planned and the publishers welcome suggestions from teachers.

EXTENDING SCIENCE 2

WATER

Selected Topics

Second Edition

E N Ramsden BSc PhD DPhil
R E Lee BSc

Stanley Thornes (Publishers) Ltd

© E N Ramsden and R E Lee 1983, 1990

All rights reserved. No part* of this publication may be reproduced or transmitted in any form or by any means, electronic or mechanical, including photocopy, recording, or any information storage and retrieval system, without permission in writing from the publisher or under licence from the Copyright Licensing Agency Limited. Further details of such licences (for reprographic reproduction) may be obtained from the Copyright Licensing Agency Limited, of 33-4 Alfred Place, London WC1E 7DP.

First published in 1983 by
Stanley Thornes (Publishers) Ltd
Old Station Drive
Leckhampton
CHELTENHAM GL53 0DN

Reprinted 1986
Reprinted 1987
Second edition 1990

*An exception is made for the word puzzles on pp. 18, 24, 31, 45 and 82. Teachers may photocopy a puzzle to save time for a pupil who would otherwise need to copy from his/her copy of the book. Teachers wishing to make multiple copies of a word puzzle for distribution to a class without individual copies of the book must apply to the publishers in the normal way.

British Library Cataloguing in Publication Data

Ramsden, E. N.
  Water.
  1. Water
  I. Title   II. Lee, R. E.   III. Series
  553.7

ISBN 0-7487-0448-5

Typeset by Tech-Set, Gateshead, Tyne & Wear.
Printed and bound in Great Britain by Ebenezer Baylis & Son, Worcester.

CONTENTS

Preface vii
Acknowledgements viii

Chapter 1 We Need Water

Can you imagine life without running water? 1
Drinking-water from river-water 3
  Case History 1 The River Thames: will the salmon return now the sewage has gone? 4
Fewer fillings with fluoride 9
  Case History 2 The million pound fluoridation case 9
Questions on fluoridation 10
How water is treated in a modern sewage-works 11
The water cycle 13
The oxygen needs of some animals 15
A question of oxygen 16
Case History 3 When Cornish water turned sour 17
Wordfinder on sewage 18
Activity 1 Study the animal life in a river 19
Activity 2 How much water do you use? 19
Activity 3 Questions for discussion 20
Activity 4 Construct a model water-purifier 21
Activity 5 Some chemical experiments on water 22
Questions on water treatment 22
Crossword on water-works and sewage-works 24

Chapter 2 Water for Agriculture

Case History 4 Damming the Nile: has Egypt done the right thing? 25
Plants and water 28
  Activity 6 Some experiments on plants and water 28
Activity 7 Questions for discussion 29
Questions on water and agriculture 30
Crossword on water and agriculture 31

Chapter 3 Water for Washing

What is soap? How does it work? 32
Detergents 34
Hard and soft water 34
Soap or detergent: Which is better? 35
  Activity 8 Construct a model water-softener 36
  Activity 9 Make a bar of soap 37
  Activity 10 Experiments on soaps and detergents 37
    (1) Which disperses dirt better — soap or detergent? 37
    (2) Which is better at making oil mix with water — soap or detergent? 38
    (3) Do soap and detergent lather in hard water? 39
    (4) Which are the most alkaline detergents? 39
    (5) Which are better — enzyme detergents or non-enzyme detergents? 40
    (6) Which detergent gives you the most for your money? 41
Questions on soaps and detergents 42
Crossword on soaps and detergents 45

Chapter 4 Pollution

Pollution by industry	46	Rivers and lakes	55
Rivers	46	Case History 7 Lake Erie:	
Case History 5 The River Irwell	46	a matter of death and life	55
Polluters of our rivers	46	Activity 11 What makes algae	
Questions on polluters	48	grow?	57
Case History 6 Pollution in the		Ground-water	58
Rhine	49	Questions on pollution by fertilisers	61
Questions on the Sandoz accident	51	Pesticides	61
Estuaries	51	Questions on pollution by agriculture	62
Mercury	52	Water privatisation	64
Pollution by sewage	53	What do you think?	65
Questions on pollution by sewage	54	Questions on water quality	65
Pollution by agriculture	54		

Chapter 5 The Boundless Sea

Cast History 8 A drop in the ocean	68	Questions on oil spills	80
What can be done?	69	Activity 12 Ways of cleaning	
No Happy New Year for the birds!	72	oil-soaked feathers	80
The North Sea	73	Questions on pollution	81
Burning waste at sea	74	Crossword on water pollution	82
Questions on pollution at sea	75	Some questions for discussion	83
Case History 9 The biggest oil		A final word: pollution and	
spill — the *Exxon Valdez*	76	conservation	83
The effects on marine life	77	What is water?	83
Methods of dealing with oil slicks	79	What is pure water?	83
Dispersants	79	What is polluted water?	83
Skimming oil off the sea	79	Why do we need to protect water	
Burning	79	from pollution?	84
Solidifying the oil	79	What is conservation?	84

How do your results compare with ours?	85	Answers to selected questions	85
		Index	87

PREFACE

We wrote the first edition of this book because the subjects of water and the pollution of water interest us. We hoped that children would find the topics which we selected interesting and come to realise the importance of conserving our environment.

The first edition of the book was used as extension material in junior chemistry courses, as part of general science courses and as background material for older pupils following certificate courses. When GCSE was introduced, teachers found that the book, in common with other titles in the Extending Science series, was a source of the new-style material in the GCSE syllabuses.

The Extending Science series began as a set of books dealing with the social, economic, environmental and technological aspects of science. Since the series began, these aspects of science have been incorporated into the National Criteria for GCSE and into the National Curriculum. Now that these social aspects of science are part of mainstream curriculum science, the Extending Science books are being used in GCSE modular science courses.

In the second edition of *Water*, we have brought topics up to date and have also included more opportunities for pupils to practise their skills in interpreting and analysing data and in devising experiments of their own. The book is not intended to provide the complete coverage of water that is required for examination courses: information and experiments that can be found readily in textbooks have been omitted.

E N Ramsden
Beverley, Humberside, 1990

R E Lee
St George's College, Weybridge, 1990

ACKNOWLEDGEMENTS

We are grateful to Mr J R Dennison and Mr B Rogers, who read the original draft and made many helpful suggestions. Miss Laura Hale has given invaluable assistance with the diagrams, and Mr D F Manley has made significant improvements in the crosswords and supplied the wordfinder. We thank our publishers for the enthusiasm and attention to detail which have gone into the production of this book, and our families for their encouragement.

The authors and publishers are grateful to the following who provided photographs and gave permission for reproduction:

Barnaby's Picture Library (p. 26); The British Oxygen Company Ltd (p. 56); Esso Petroleum Company Ltd (p. 70 bottom); Donald Innes (p. 6 centre, bottom, p. 13 top); Mansell Collection (pp. 2, 5); Northumbrian Water Authority (p. 3); Oxford Scientific Films (p. 77); Popperfoto (p. 25, p. 68); Robert Roskrow Photography (p. 69); Ian Ross (p. 8); Syndication International (p. 70 top); Thames Water Authority (p. 7); Wessex Water Authority (p. 13 bottom); Yorkshire Water Authority (p. 6 top).

CHAPTER 1
WE NEED WATER

CAN YOU IMAGINE LIFE WITHOUT RUNNING WATER?

We use plenty of water. The sketches below show some ways in which we use water. No doubt you will be able to think of many more.

What use is water?

We use more water for washing than people did a century ago. We each use 50 litres (10 gallons) a day for flushing the toilet. Our homes, schools and factories need a plentiful supply of water. Where does it all come from? The water we use comes from rivers and lakes to reservoirs for storage. From these, it goes to water-works to be made fit to be piped into our homes. Used water passes from our buildings to sewer pipes. These lead to a sewage-works. Here, waste water is purified and returned to a river. To appreciate what the water-works and sewage-works do for us, we need to look into the history books.

In the nineteenth century, only rich people had water laid on to their houses. Poorer people often collected rain-water in tubs beside their houses. The rain had fallen through smoke and grime, and collected more dirt while in the tub. Some people had wells and pumped water from them up to street level. The well-water could be fouled by water seeping into it from a nearby cesspit. (A cesspit was what the toilets emptied into.)

Most of the water for town dwellers came from water companies. In London, some of these took water from the River Thames and pumped it without any treatment along the mains to streets or houses. Since the sewers emptied into the Thames, the companies were selling diluted sewage as drinking-water! This led to disease. The dreadful diseases of cholera, typhoid, tuberculosis and smallpox were common.

A stand-pipe in 1860

The water was supplied to a stand-pipe in the street for a few hours a day. There were so many houses to each stand-pipe that a crowd of people would rush to get water when the supply was turned on. Often, they had no time to collect enough for their needs. They could not hope to keep clean. They had insufficient water to wash their clothes or themselves, and they smelled horrible.

Outside London, there were some better water companies. Some filtered water through beds of sand and gravel before pumping it to the people.

Things are very different now. A modern water-works is very careful to make the water fit to drink.

DRINKING-WATER FROM RIVER-WATER

Water is taken from rivers and reservoirs in tunnels to the treatment works. There it is made fit to drink. The photograph below shows the Kielder Reservoir and Dam in Northumbria, which were opened in 1982. Seven miles long and half a mile wide, the reservoir is the largest man-made lake in Europe. The reservoir holds 200 billion litres of water, and supplies 1000 million litres a day to the homes and industries of north-eastern England. The surrounding countryside is being developed as a recreation area.

Kielder Reservoir and Dam

The next illustration shows the treatment which reservoir-water receives. Rubbish is removed, solid material is allowed to settle, and the water is filtered. Chlorine is added to kill germs, and the water is fit to drink.

A water-treatment works

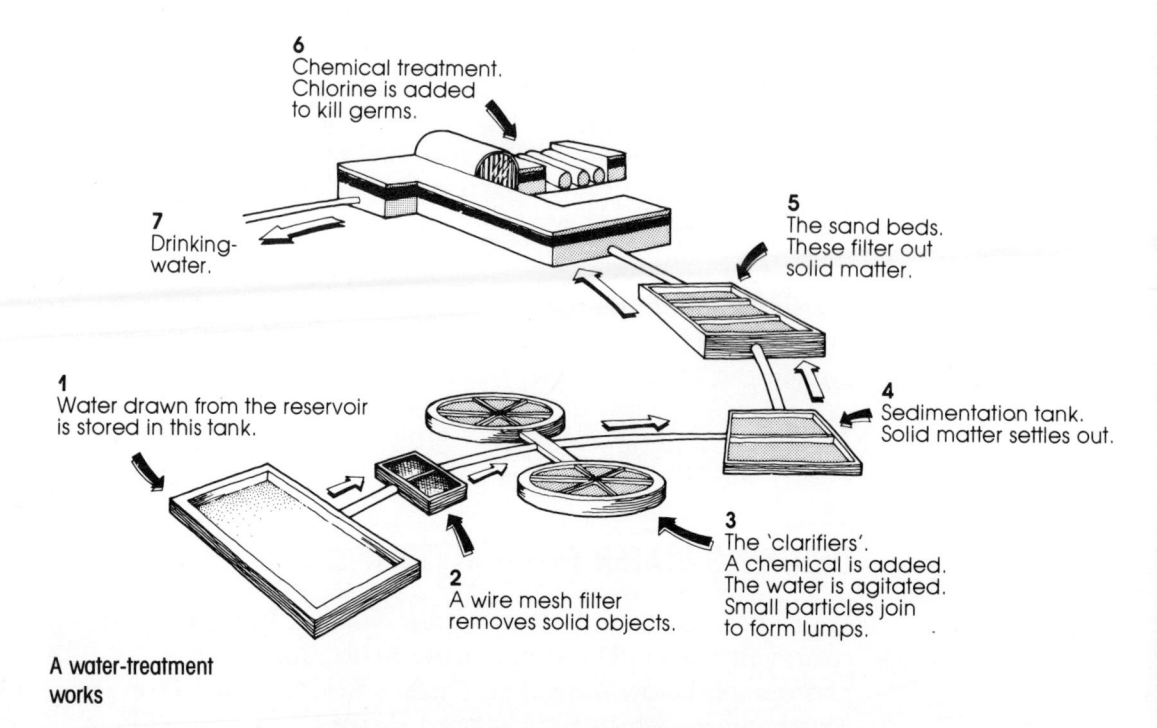

1. Water drawn from the reservoir is stored in this tank.
2. A wire mesh filter removes solid objects.
3. The 'clarifiers'. A chemical is added. The water is agitated. Small particles join to form lumps.
4. Sedimentation tank. Solid matter settles out.
5. The sand beds. These filter out solid matter.
6. Chemical treatment. Chlorine is added to kill germs.
7. Drinking-water.

Some of the water we use comes from underground sources. This water does not need the complete treatment. It is simply pumped out of the ground and chlorinated.

CASE HISTORY 1

The River Thames: will the salmon return now the sewage has gone?

The Thames rises in high ground and flows to the sea. Over the 70 mile stretch from Teddington to the North Sea, the Thames is tidal. It ebbs and flows with the North Sea. For this reason, any pollutants in the Thames are not washed out to sea but float to and fro with the tide. As pollution increases, the number of fish that can live in the river decreases. Until about 1750, there were salmon in the Thames. They need plenty of dissolved oxygen in the water. From 1750 onwards, pollution became more and more severe, and the level of dissolved oxygen fell. The reason for this was the expansion of London.

More and more people were living in London, and there was more and more human waste to dispose of. Only wealthy people had a lavatory in the house. The poor had a 'privy' shared between several houses. The privy was a shed with a wooden seat inside, below which was a cesspit. When the cesspit was full, it had to be emptied by workmen. They wheeled the unpleasant contents of the cesspit away in carts. The people who did this job were called 'nightmen'. Why do you think they were made to do this job at night?

People with houses on the river banks built privies overhanging the water so that they would empty straight into the river. If you look at the drawing below, you will see the privies alongside the river.

Underground sewers had been built since 1550, to carry away rain-water. They were not originally intended to take away refuse. When the water-closet was invented, the contents of the toilet were washed by a stream of water into a cesspit outside the house. As the problem of emptying the cesspits grew, the toilets were discharged into drains running into street sewers, and then, without any treatment, into the Thames. Bacteria in the river broke down the sewage in the water into harmless substances.

Old houses in London Street, Dockhead, about 1810

The Metropolitan Commissioners of Sewers were founded in 1843. They liked the mysterious way in which the river disposed of their sewage. (Bacteria are still a mystery to some people!) They did away with 200 000 smelly cesspits. Water-closets took over, and their contents were drained into the river. Bacteria multiplied, feeding on this sewage. Much of the oxygen in the water was used up by the bacteria. Some bacteria became short of oxygen, and died. The remaining bacteria could not cope with all the sewage, and the sewage content of the river increased. It was carried to and fro on the tide. When it reached Westminster, the Members of Parliament found the stench unbearable. They debated methods of dealing with the nuisance, but could not agree on a course of action. Meanwhile, germs were breeding in the sewage.

(a) Aeration tanks, (b) and (c) filter beds in a modern sewage-works

The Thames water was used as drinking-water. Such foul water was the cause of several epidemics. Epidemics of cholera broke out in 1831, killing 7000 people, and in 1848, killing 15 000 people. Parliament decided to try to get rid of the sewage.

The Metropolitan Board of Works was founded in 1855. The Board had the sewage carried in large sewers down to two reservoirs 30 miles downstream of London Bridge. These large reservoirs held the sewage and released it when the tide went out. The hope was that the river would carry all the sewage out to sea. The huge volume of sewage was too much, however, and the river could not cope with it.

In 1880, they began to treat sewage with lime. The treatment was carried out in covered channels. The solids which settled to the bottom of the channels were carried out to sea in ships and dumped. The liquid from the channels was discharged into the river. The population continued to expand, and the river continued to be foul. Around 1890, a man called Dibden had the brilliant idea of arranging for living organisms to feed on the sewage. He allowed sewage to trickle through towers filled with coke. The coke contained plenty of air, and bacteria grew in the towers and fed on the sewage. Dibden had invented the biological filter method of purification which is still in use today. The photographs opposite show aeration tanks and filter beds in a modern sewage-works.

In 1930, a huge new sewage-works for the whole of London was built at Mogden. Bacteria were used to break down the sewage to harmless products. In 1964, the big plant at Crossness opened, and started to treat 500 million litres of sewage a day. Beckton sewage-works opened 10 years later. The photograph below shows a scene in the laboratories of Beckton Works. Samples are taken and analysed at all stages of treatment.

Laboratory in Beckton sewage-works

The improvement in the Thames was spectacular. The graph below shows how the level of dissolved oxygen shot up after 1964.

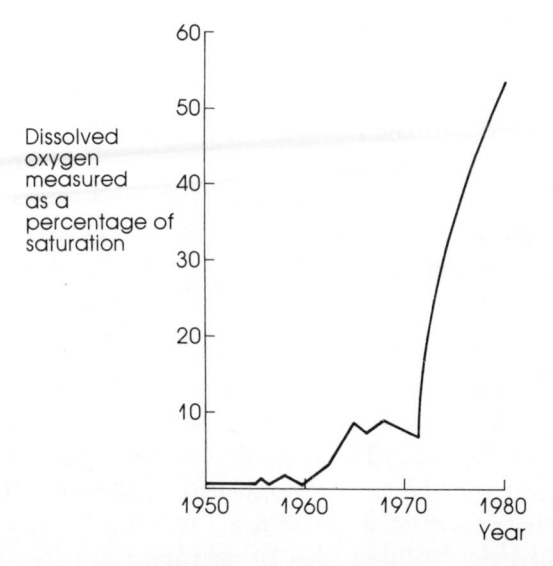

The level of dissolved oxygen in the Thames

Fish started to return from the sea to the river. Plaice, herring, sole and 40 other kinds of fish are now found in the Thames. Formerly, only the eel, which can survive in foul water, was found. Will the salmon ever return to the Thames? To find out, scientists have put marked salmon into the river. They swim downstream to the sea. If they return, they will be identified by their markings. Then we shall know that the Thames is clean again. It would be a fitting end to the success story of the Thames! The photograph below shows someone enjoying their leisure on the Thames (he fell off immediately after the photograph was taken!).

Recreation on the Thames

FEWER FILLINGS WITH FLUORIDE

In 1985, the UK Government passed a law to allow water authorities to add sodium fluoride to drinking-water. Over a period of 40 years, dentists had noticed that children from some parts of the country suffered less from tooth decay than children from other regions. Research workers made the connection between a high level of fluoride in the water of a region and a low rate of tooth decay. Fluorides have the biggest effect on the teeth of children up to the age of 8 years. It seemed so simple to add fluoride to the drinking-water. Children would then have fewer cavities and fewer extractions. Many people, however, were against the addition of fluoride to their water supply. They were worried because large amounts of fluoride can damage teeth. It can cause *fluorosis* which makes bones brittle and damages teeth (see Extending Science 1: *Air*). The level of fluoride in drinking-water must be carefully controlled. Water companies add enough sodium fluoride to bring the concentration of fluoride in the water up to 1 p.p.m. (part per million). Some Water companies think that fluoridation of the water supply is too risky. They suggest that people use a toothpaste containing a fluoride instead.

Teeth are covered with a sticky layer called *plaque*. It contains bacteria and sugars. When the bacteria feed on the sugars, they produce acids. When these acids attack tooth enamel, teeth start to decay. The enamel of teeth is a compound called hydroxyapatite. Fluorides convert hydroxyapatite into fluoroapatite. This is even less soluble than the original enamel. It is better at resisting attack by acids, because the basic hydroxide part of the compound has been replaced by fluoride.

CASE HISTORY 2

The million pound fluoridation case

In September, 1978, Strathclyde Regional Council, in Scotland, decided that they wished to add fluoride to their water supply. As other regions in the UK already had fluoridated water, Strathclyde did not foresee difficulty. They had not reckoned on Mrs Catherine McColl, who was determined to stop the plans for fluoridation. In October, 1978, she was granted legal aid in her fight against fluoridation. This meant that she could take Strathclyde Council to court, and her legal fees would be paid. Mrs McColl said that fluoridation is ineffective, unsafe and illegal. Experts came from far and wide to testify. Lord Jauncy sat as judge. The case started on 23

September, 1980, and ended on 26 July, 1982, after 200 days of sitting. This was the longest and costliest case in Scottish legal history. It cost the taxpayer £1 million. On 29 June, 1983, the judge gave his 400 page verdict. Lord Jauncy said that he was not impressed by the evidence presented by Dr Yiamouyannis and Dr Burke against fluoridation. He said that Dr Yiamouyannis 'not infrequently allowed his hostility to fluoridation to obscure his scientific judgement'. He said that Dr Burke's evidence of cancer caused by fluoride in the USA was 'vague and unimpressive'. Lord Jauncy was impressed by the evidence in favour of fluoridation given by Professor Newell, Sir Richard Doll, Dr Sharrett and Dr Erikson. He said that their evidence 'appeared to me to be based on sound scientific principles'. The judge decided that fluoridation is both safe and effective. There was a sting in the tail of this judgement. The judge said that it was beyond his powers, however, to order Stathclyde to fluoridate their water supply. Mrs McColl had succeeded in stopping the fluoridation of Strathclyde water! But her triumph was not to last.

The decision was very widely debated. The water authorities did not know whether or not they were entitled to fluoridate water. The Government decided to act to clarify the situation. In 1985, a new Act of Parliament gave water authorities the right to fluoridate water supplies if they wish.

QUESTIONS ON FLUORIDATION

1 Do you think tax payers' money should have been spent on Mrs McColl's case? Give reasons for your answer.

2 What did the judge say about the quality of the scientific evidence presented by witnesses?

3 How long did the judge take to consider his verdict?

4 How long did Mrs McColl have to wait from her original complaint until the final verdict?

5 State what you think are the good points and the bad points in this case.

6 Explain why both sides could claim victory after the case. Say how the situation was finally clarified.

7 Table A shows the results of three national surveys (British Fluoridation Society Action Report, 1987). The question was, 'Do you think fluoride should be added to water if it can reduce tooth decay?'

Table A: Responses to national surveys (as percentages)

Response	National opinion poll, market research 1980 (%)	Gallup poll, 1985 (%)	Gallup poll, 1987 (%)
Yes	66.5	71	76
No	15.8	17	15
Don't know	17.7	11	9

(a) Comment on the way that opinion on the question of fluoridation has changed over the years.
(b) Suggest why the percentage of 'don't knows' has decreased over the years.

Table B shows responses obtained in local surveys by health authorities.

Table B: Responses to the question of fluoridation (as percentages)

Response	North West, 1985 (%)	Mersey, 1986 (%)	West Midlands, 1980–84 (%)
Yes	75	77	64
No	15	15	27
Don't know	10	8	9

(c) Which of the local surveys can you compare with a national survey for the same year? How good is the agreement between them?
(d) The surveys of the North-West and the Mersey were only one year apart. How close is the agreement between them?
(e) Is it fair to compare the West Midlands' figures for 1980–84 with the Mersey's figures for 1986? Explain your answer.

HOW WATER IS TREATED IN A MODERN SEWAGE-WORKS

A sewage-works prepares water for returning to a river. The stages of treatment are shown in the diagram overleaf.

The water discharged into the river looks clear. It contains a little suspended matter, some dissolved chemicals and some germs. Bacteria in the river purify the water. There must be enough oxygen dissolved in the water to keep the bacteria alive. If the river becomes too poor in oxygen, the bacteria die, and the sewage content of the water increases.

The sewage-works

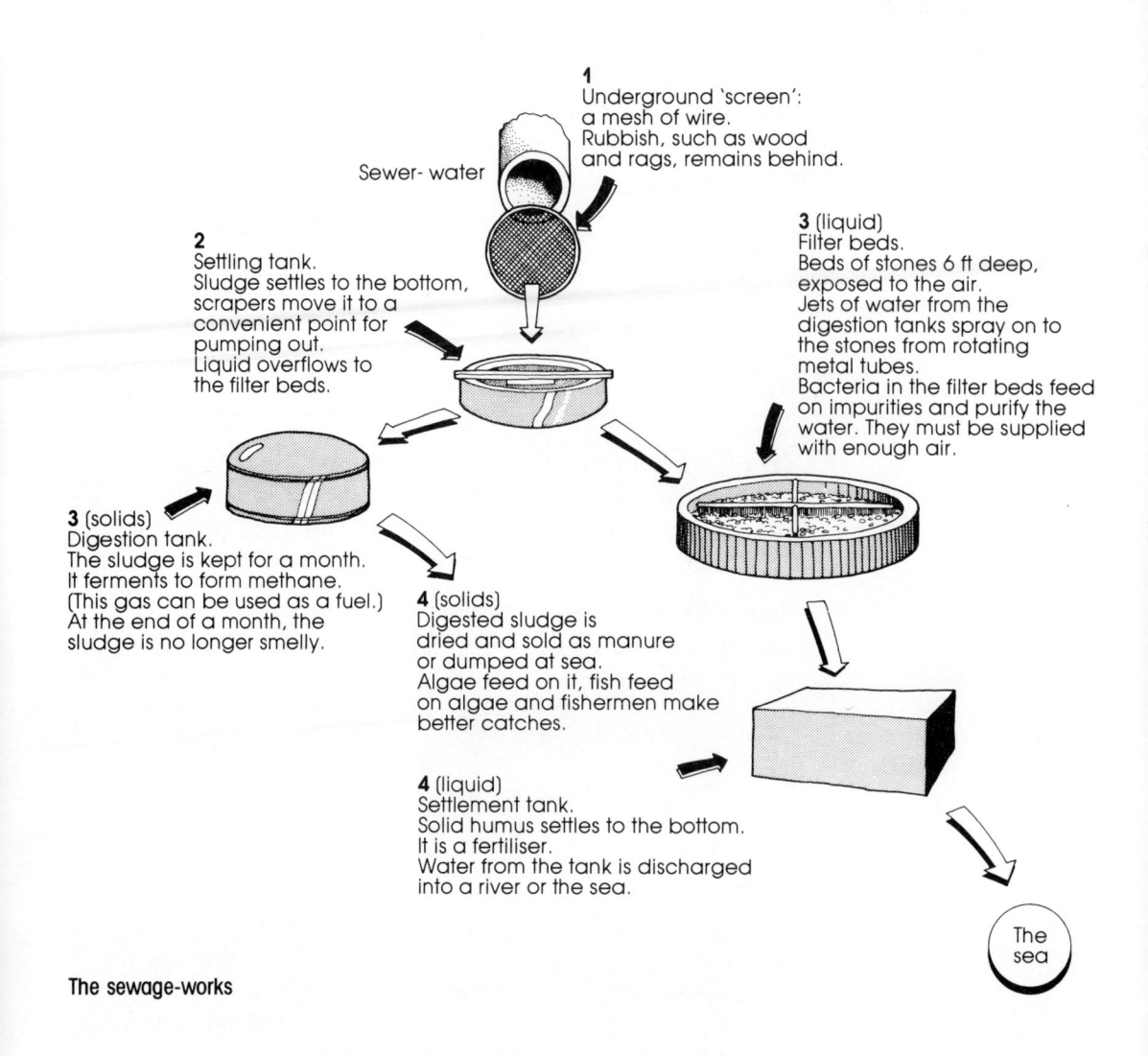

1 Underground 'screen': a mesh of wire. Rubbish, such as wood and rags, remains behind.

Sewer-water

2 Settling tank. Sludge settles to the bottom, scrapers move it to a convenient point for pumping out. Liquid overflows to the filter beds.

3 (liquid) Filter beds. Beds of stones 6 ft deep, exposed to the air. Jets of water from the digestion tanks spray on to the stones from rotating metal tubes. Bacteria in the filter beds feed on impurities and purify the water. They must be supplied with enough air.

3 (solids) Digestion tank. The sludge is kept for a month. It ferments to form methane. (This gas can be used as a fuel.) At the end of a month, the sludge is no longer smelly.

4 (solids) Digested sludge is dried and sold as manure or dumped at sea. Algae feed on it, fish feed on algae and fishermen make better catches.

4 (liquid) Settlement tank. Solid humus settles to the bottom. It is a fertiliser. Water from the tank is discharged into a river or the sea.

The sea

The photographs opposite show the sedimentation tanks (or settling tanks) at a sewage-works, and a sludge ship, used to carry sludge out to sea for dumping.

Not all sewage is treated at sewage-works. Untreated sewage is still discharged into rivers and the sea. Sewage is made up of compounds which contain carbon, hydrogen and oxygen, some nitrogen and some sulphur. All of these are oxidised by oxygen to harmless compounds. None of these oxidation products is unpleasant or smelly. If too much sewage is present in water, all the oxygen is used up. The sewage is then attacked by different bacteria, which do not need oxygen. They turn sewage into methane, CH_4, and the smelly gases, ammonia, NH_3 (the 'nappies' smell), and hydrogen sulphide, H_2S (the 'bad eggs' smell). Thus, in the absence of oxygen, unpleasant decay products are formed. The presence of dissolved oxygen in the water is all-important.

Sedimentation tanks

Sludge ship

THE WATER CYCLE

Nature provides us with fresh water. Rain-water seeps through the ground and collects in streams, rivers and lakes for us to use. Trees draw in water through their roots. After they have extracted the useful salts from the water, they pass water vapour out of their leaves. This process is called *transpiration*. Animals drink water from streams and rivers. The water they excrete passes back to the soil, and the water vapour they breathe out puts water back into circulation.

The warmth of the Sun causes evaporation of water from rivers, lakes and seas. Water vapour passes upwards, until it reaches cooler air and condenses to form clouds of tiny droplets of water. When the clouds are cooled, they release water as rain. This cycle of events is called the *water cycle*.

The diagram below shows how we modify the water cycle. Water is taken from the river to a water-treatment works. From here, it is supplied to houses and factories. After use, it goes to the sewage-works. After treatment at the sewage-works, it is pure enough to be discharged into the sea.

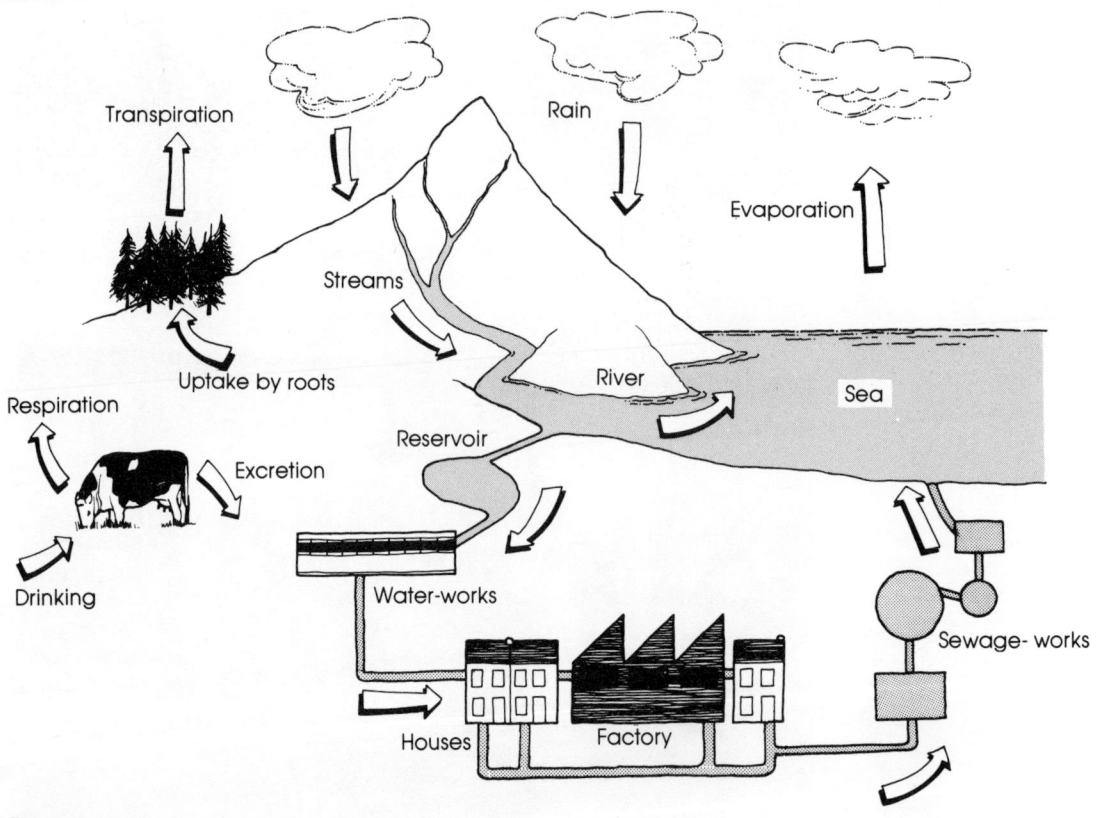

The water cycle

Not every country can take safe water for granted as most of us can in the United Kingdom. In many poor countries, children are dying through drinking infected water. In some countries, the drinking water is polluted by sewage as it was in the United Kingdom 200 years ago. The World Health Organization has figures to show that 80 per cent of all the disease in the world is linked with water. In 1980, the United Nations set itself a target date of 1990. By that year, the UN hoped to have safe water and sanitation in every country.

Water contains dissolved air. This is very important as it allows fish and other water animals to breathe. Air is more soluble in cold water than in hot water. If water is warmed up, dissolved air will come out of solution. If a river becomes

Does this water look polluted?

too warm, fish find they have less dissolved oxygen to breathe. Some industries need water for cooling purposes. They take water from a river, use it to cool their plant, and return it to the river. A plant which uses a great deal of water for cooling is a nuclear power plant. This can warm up a river by several degrees. It results in less air being available for fish. This problem has not occurred in the United Kingdom. It is more likely to happen in warmer climates. It is called *thermal pollution*, and is most serious when it occurs in rivers which are already short of oxygen on account of some other form of pollution.

THE OXYGEN NEEDS OF SOME ANIMALS

If waste materials are put into a stream or river, they damage the plant and animal life in the water. The water is said to be *polluted*. Some factories discharge waste into rivers. Sewage is another pollutant which is discharged into rivers. Sewage decays gradually to form harmless substances. Dissolved oxygen is used in the decay process. If there is not enough oxygen in the water, decay cannot take place. Sewage then accumulates, and the water becomes foul. The degree of pollution of river water is often measured by its *biochemical oxygen demand (BOD)*. This is the mass of oxygen used up by a one litre sample of the water in a fixed period of time. The higher the BOD, the more polluted is the water.

To find out whether the water in a river is rich or poor in oxygen, you can look at the animals in the river. The diagram at the top of the next page shows some aquatic (water-dwelling)

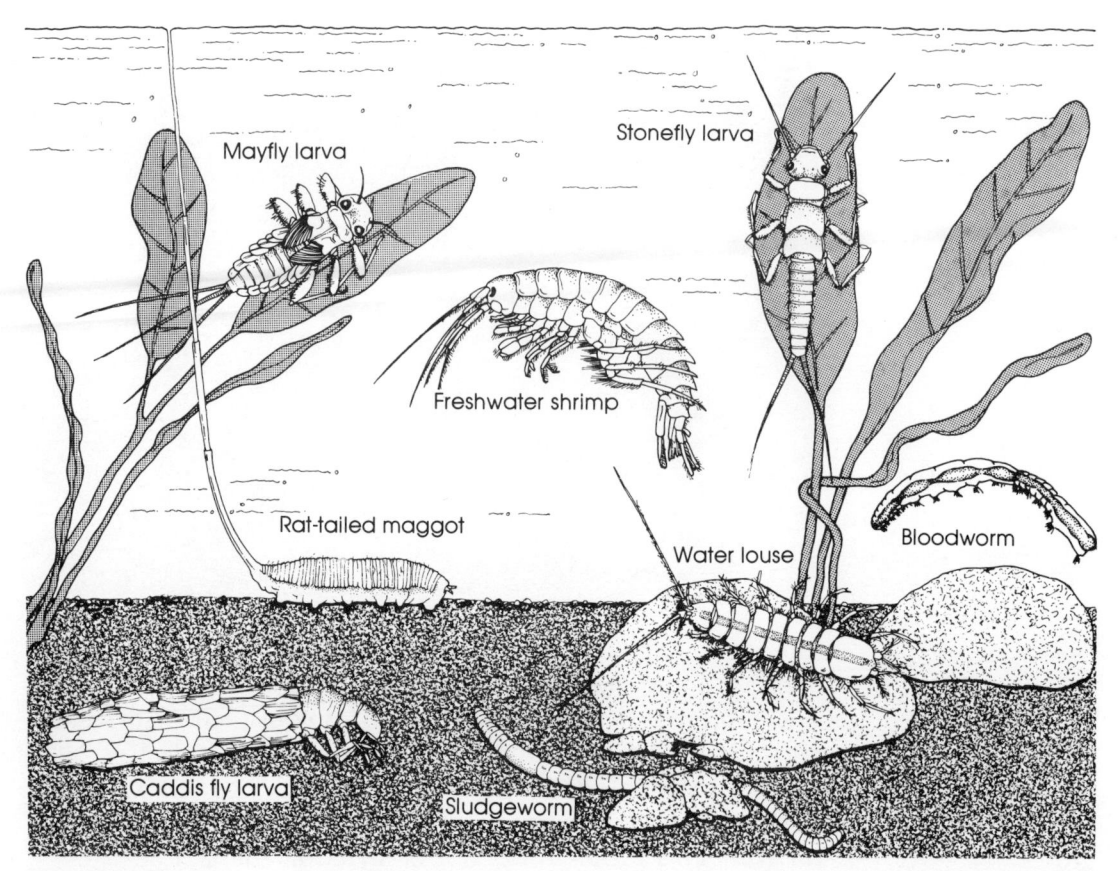

Some aquatic animals

animals. The rat-tailed maggot can survive in water containing very little dissolved oxygen because it breathes air from the surface of the water through a long air tube. The little red sludgeworm can also survive in polluted water as it feeds on decaying plants. If these are the only animals you can find, you know the water is highly polluted. The bright-red bloodworm and the water louse can survive in fairly polluted water as they feed on decaying plants. If the grey freshwater shrimp and the caddis fly larva are found, then you know the degree of pollution is slight. These animals need more oxygen than the worms and need fresh plants to feed on. If you can see the stonefly larva and the mayfly larva, then you know the water is clean, because these animals cannot live in polluted water.

A QUESTION OF OXYGEN

The following table shows the solubility of oxygen (the volume of oxygen dissolved in 1 kg of water) at different temperatures.

Temperature (°C)	0	5	10	15	20	25	30
Solubility of oxygen (cm^3/kg of water)	10.2	8.9	7.9	7.0	6.4	5.8	5.3

(a) On graph paper, make a plot of solubility (on the vertical axis) against temperature (on the horizontal axis).

(b) Explain why the fish in a pond become less active during hot weather.

(c) Fish also become less active during very cold weather. Can you explain this?

CASE HISTORY 3

When Cornish water turned sour

The idea of blondes having their hair turned green by something nasty in the water may seem quite funny. For 20 000 people in North Cornwall in 1988, however, the 'something nasty in the water' was no laughing matter. There were worse complaints than green hair. They suffered from burnt and blistered mouths, sickness, diarrhoea and rashes.

Many suffered from exhaustion, inability to concentrate and memory loss. Tim Wheater is a classical musician who used to play the flute. He was formerly a member of the Eurythmics pop group. He suffered ulceration of his gums and partial paralysis of his upper lip. He can no longer play the flute and has lost his profession and his income.

The pollution of the water was caused by aluminium sulphate, 20 tonnes of an 8 per cent solution of it. This solution should have been pumped into a storage tank. Instead it was pumped by mistake into a reservoir at the water treatment works. Plant engineers realised the water was acidic. They flushed out the water mains; this action killed over 30 000 fish, mainly young trout, in local rivers. It took the engineers 48 hours to realise the full extent of the crisis. The acidic water attacked the scale on the inside of hot-water systems. Copper salts in the scale dissolved in the drinking-water. Levels were 7 times the European Community limits for copper salts in drinking-water. Most of the symptoms suffered by consumers could have been caused by copper salts. The health of those affected will be watched over a period of years. A connection has been discovered between aluminium in the drinking-water and Alzheimer's disease, a form of mental illness.

WORDFINDER ON SEWAGE

Copy out (or photocopy) the grid below and then see if you can find answers to the 26 clues. One has been ringed and you can ring the other 25. Three of the answers each consist of two words. The words read from right to left or from left to right horizontally and from top to bottom or from bottom to top vertically. Do not write on this page.

1 London river (6)
2 It swam in 1 until about 1750 (6)
3 The level of dissolved ___ in 1 went up after 1964 (6)
4 It goes over 1 (6, 6)
5 They emptied cesspits (8)
6 This disease killed 15 000 people in London in 1848 (7)
7 They can break down sewage (8)
8 He invented a way of dealing with sewage (6)
9 They need very little 3 (4)
10 A gas that smells of nappies (7)
11 A sewage-works for London was built at ___ in 1930 (6) ...
12 ... and another one at ___ in 1964 (9) ...
13 ... ___ sewage-works opened 10 years later (7)
14 You get buckets of water from this (4)
15 Part of a modern sewage-works (8, 4) ...
16 ... where ___ goes to the bottom (6)
17 A gas from sewage with the formula CH_4 (7)
18 Water is purified in the ___ beds of a sewage-works (6)
19, 20 A gas that smells of bad eggs (8, 8: two words in different places)
21, 22 If a river warms up by several degrees there is less ___ available for ___ (3, 4: two words in different places)
23 In the formula NH_3, N stands for ___ (8)
24 In the formula CH_4, C stands for ___ (6)
25 At one time sewage was carried out to ___ and dumped (3)
26 An essential part of the water cycle (4)

T	H	A	M	E	S	N	E	G	O	R	D	Y	H
C	S	L	C	A	R	B	O	N	S	D	W	N	A
B	I	B	A	C	T	E	R	I	A	I	L	I	K
A	F	O	S	L	U	D	G	E	L	B	O	G	N
I	C	M	F	I	L	T	E	R	M	D	N	H	A
N	L	O	T	N	E	G	Y	X	O	E	D	T	T
O	T	G	I	R	W	E	L	L	N	N	O	M	G
M	X	D	B	D	E	M	E	T	H	A	N	E	N
M	B	E	C	K	T	O	N	W	S	M	B	N	I
A	A	N	N	N	U	P	S	N	I	A	R	M	L
D	E	I	A	C	H	O	L	E	R	A	I	S	T
G	S	L	I	Z	S	U	L	P	H	I	D	E	T
N	I	T	R	O	G	E	N	M	P	O	G	A	E
S	L	E	E	D	C	R	O	S	S	N	E	S	S

| ACTIVITY 1 | **Study the animal life in a river** |

An interesting activity is to carry out a study of a river in your area. The animals you find (see p. 16) will tell you how clean or polluted the water is. You will need a net and a magnifying glass and instructions from your teacher.

| ACTIVITY 2 | **How much water do you use?** |

Have you any idea how much water you use in a day? We suggest you tackle this activity at home.

1) Find out how much water is needed for each of the following uses:
   (a) filling a kettle
   (b) filling a watering can
   (c) cooking a meal
   (d) half-filling a bath
   (e) filling a sink with enough water for washing-up.

Check your answers against those on p. 85. These are given in litres and gallons; 1 gallon (8 pints) is 4.5 litres.

2) Say how much water you think the average person uses each day for:
   (a) cooking and drinking
   (b) washing and bathing
   (c) laundry
   (d) flushing the lavatory
   (e) gardening
   (f) dishwashing.

   Compare your answers with those on p. 85. The Water Boards tell us that each person uses about 140 litres (31 gallons) a day.

3) Have you a tap that drips? Put a measuring jug under the tap. Find out how much water comes from the tap in 10 minutes. Calculate how much water comes from the tap in 24 hours.
   The Water Boards reckon that waste from dripping taps and leaking pipes takes 20 litres (4.4 gallons) a day of the 140 litres (31 gallons) we use.

ACTIVITY 3

Questions for discussion

We suggest that you may like to tackle this work in small groups. Then you can pool ideas.

1) Some people suggest that it would be a good idea to have water-meters in houses. These would measure the amount of water that house used. Then the family would be charged for the water they had used. The idea is to make people more careful in their use of water. Do you think it is a good idea? Would it be a fair scheme? Can you see any disadvantages?

2) Imagine that very little rain falls this summer. Your town is running short of water. If you were in charge, what restrictions would you make on the use of water to make the supply last as long as possible?

3) Make a list of all the things you use water for in your home.

4) Make a list of the industries in your nearest town. How many of them are big users of water?

5) Water is used for recreation. Many sports involve water. Rivers, lakes, reservoirs and the sea are all used for recreation. Make a list of water sports. For each sport, say what kind of water is needed and whether the sport will pollute the water.

6) What use can be made of reservoirs for recreation? Bear in mind the need to avoid polluting the water in the reservoir.

7) Think of a lake or a river or a stretch of coastline near you. Describe how you would develop the area for recreation. Make a plan of the area. Describe any roads, buildings, car-parks, etc., that would be needed.

8) Farming is an industry. What type of farming is carried on in your area? Is the rainfall high or low in the area? What type of farming is carried on in areas of (a) high rainfall, (b) low rainfall?

9) Water is used for transport. See what information you can obtain about the importance of rivers and canals for transport. What are the advantages and disadvantages of transporting people and cargoes by water?

10) Water is used for defence. How many examples can you think of in which people have used water as a means of protection?

ACTIVITY 4

Construct a model water-purifier

The diagram below shows one possible model. It is made from a plastic orangeade bottle, from which the bottom has been cut out. The neck is fitted with a rubber bung with a piece of glass tubing through it. The bottle is filled with a layer of large clean stones, then a layer of washed gravel, and finally a layer of washed sand. When muddy water is poured into the top, it should come out of the bottom clean.

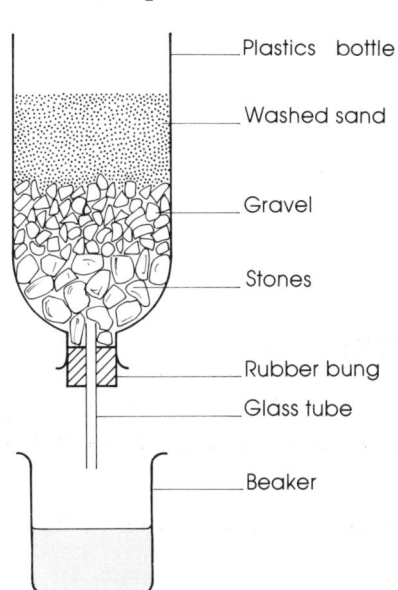

A model water-purifier

| ACTIVITY 5 | **Some chemical experiments on water** |

To do these experiments, you need to obtain water from as many different sources as possible. Examples are:

Rain-water	Water from a stream
Tap-water	Water from a stagnant pond
Sea-water	Water from a river in the countryside
Distilled water	Water from a river in the town

Ask your teacher for practical instructions to help you answer the following questions. The different types of water will give different results. The answers will tell you how pure the different types of water are.

1) How much undissolved solid material is present in the water? (Filtration will tell you.)

2) How much dissolved solid is present in the water? (Evaporation will tell you.)

3) Is there dissolved air present in the water? (Warming the water will bring air out of solution.)

4) Is the water acidic or alkaline or neutral? (Universal indicator will tell you.)

QUESTIONS ON WATER TREATMENT

1 Imagine there is a drought, and you and your family have to cut down on water. How could you halve your consumption of water? What is the last thing you would cut down on? What is the first thing you would cut down on?

2 What do people mean when they say that water is 'polluted'? Why is it safe to discharge a small amount of sewage into a river? What is there in the water that is able to break down sewage into harmless products?

3 The term 'water cycle' describes the processes which put water vapour into the air and the processes which take water vapour out of the air. Name two processes which put water vapour into the air. Name two processes which put water into the soil.

4 Where does mains water come from? Where is it stored before treatment? What is done to remove bits of rubbish from the water? How are very small objects removed? What is the name of the living organisms which cannot be removed? What harm is there in letting them remain in the water? What is done about them?

5 'Waterfacts 1986' (Combined Water Authorities of England and Wales) published the following figures.

Average use of water per head per day (%) *(Total = 130 litres/head/day)*	
Bath or shower	17
WC	32
Washing-machine	12
Dishwasher	1
Miscellaneous	35
Outside	3

Average use of drinking-water per head per day (%) *(Total = 1.6 litres/head/day)*	
Tea	37
Coffee	12
Cold water	6
Alcohol	13
Cordial	4
Other	28

(a) Show the two sets of figures as bar charts or as pie charts.
(b) Calculate the volume of water used by a family of four for baths or showers in one week.
(c) Calculate the volume of water used to make tea for a family of five for one month (30 days).

6 What organisms cause sewage to break down? These organisms multiply if the amount of sewage in the water increases. How does this multiplication lead to their destruction? What do they run short of, and what happens to them? What measures can be taken to prevent the destruction of these organisms?

7 If sewage decays in the absence of oxygen, three gases are formed. One is a flammable gas, which can be used as a fuel. One has a 'nappies' smell, and the third has a 'bad eggs' smell. What are these three gases?

CROSSWORD ON WATER-WORKS AND SEWAGE-WORKS

First, trace this grid on to a piece of paper (or photocopy this page). Then fill in the answers. Do not write on this page.

Across

2. Washing-machines put these into the water (4)
4. These small creatures destroy sewage (8)
7. Please ___ when people are talking about pollution (6)
8. The water ___ was much better than the 11 across (6)
9. A home uses ___ gallons of water a day for flushing the toilet (3)
10. They form an entrance for the water you drink (4)
11. An old-fashioned toilet (5)
15. Treat water with this to make it safe to drink (8)
16. People could not do this safely in the Thames 50 years ago (4)
19. Thank you (2)
20. You can store water in this (4)
21. A ___-pipe supplies water (5)
22. The water-closet may be in the smallest ___ (4)
23. Large amount of water are stored in these (10)

Down

1. This takes waste water away (5)
2. This fish will live only in clean rivers (6)
3. You can do this to get very pure water (6)
4. Opposite of front (4)
5. A dreadful disease spread by foul water (7)
6. When you ___, you lose water through the skin (8)
9. Another dreadful disease spread by foul water (7)
12. This form of water consists of tiny little droplets (4)
13. Water ___ easily from one container to another (5)
14. These are used to take solid matter out of water (7)
17. No one should ___ water (5)
18. You can ___ the surface of water to remove floating objects (4)

CHAPTER 2
WATER FOR AGRICULTURE

CASE HISTORY 4

Damming the Nile: has Egypt done the right thing?

'Egypt is the Nile; the Nile is Egypt.' This well-worn saying is a tribute to the importance of the River Nile in the economy of Egypt. Without the Nile flowing through it, Egypt would be a barren desert. Because of the Nile, Egypt has a belt of farmland running alongside each bank of the Nile. Every year, the winter rainfall swells the river. Every year, the Nile used to flood, and the flood waters brought life to the parched land.

The Nile in flood

In 1960, the Egyptian government decided to build a huge dam across the Nile. The idea was to prevent the Nile flooding by holding the water back in a lake called Lake Nasser. The water from the lake could then be channelled to the farmland gradually, instead of all at once. The Dam took 10 years and half a billion pounds to build. It is called the Aswan High Dam, and is one of the greatest engineering achievements in the world. It is more than 2 miles wide, 1000 metres thick at the base and 100 metres high. It was designed by West German engineers, and built with Russian aid.

Lake Nasser is 300 miles long. The waters of Lake Nasser have improved a million acres of land. They guarantee farmers a steady water supply by holding back heavy floods. They provide a reserve for dry years. In 1972 and 1983–85, when other African countries such as Ethiopia suffered from drought, Egyptian farmers had the water from Lake Nasser.

The Aswan High Dam

Another benefit which Egypt derives from the Aswan High Dam is electricity. At the Dam, there is an electricity generating station. The pressure of the water behind the Dam is used to drive generators. Half of Egypt's electrical power comes from the Aswan High Dam.

This massive tinkering with Nature has had some side-effects. One serious problem concerns the Nile silt. The Nile contains fine particles of solid, or silt. The silt contains minerals which enrich the soil. All the silt is now trapped behind the Dam. No longer does the Nile carry this fertiliser to the farmlands on its banks. Before the Dam was built, the flood waters of the Nile carried fertile silt to 6 million acres. This vast area now needs artificial fertilisers. Some of these must be imported. A substitute has to be found for the lost silt. No one has yet found a substitute for water!

Another problem is that the sodium chloride (common salt) content of the soil on the banks of the river has increased. In past years, it was washed out by flood waters. Now it builds up. Many crops do not like a high salt content, and yields are low.

There has been another alarming result of building the Dam. The Egyptians suffer from a tropical disease called bilharzia. It is caused by tiny worms, attacking the intestines and bladder. It is very unpleasant, causing stomach pains and damage to the liver, lungs and heart. It often shortens the victim's life. There has been a 20 per cent increase in the disease since the Dam was built. The reason is that the disease is carried by a snail which cannot survive in fast-flowing water but thrives in the irrigation canals. The whole of the 330 mile long Lake Nasser is infested with the snail, and it has spread to the canals. A person with the disease can put larvae into the water. The farmworkers work knee deep in the canals, irrigating their fields. They bathe in the canals, do laundry in the canals, and children swim in the canals. The larvae settle on a snail, and hatch into the adult flukes (tiny worms). These can infect anyone wading in the canal. Thus the disease spreads rapidly. It has always been a big problem in Egypt. Half or three-quarters of farmworkers have it. There has been a serious increase since the Dam was built. So far, there is no answer to the problem. Victims of the disease can be cured, but if they go back to the fields and start wading in the canal again, they become re-infected.

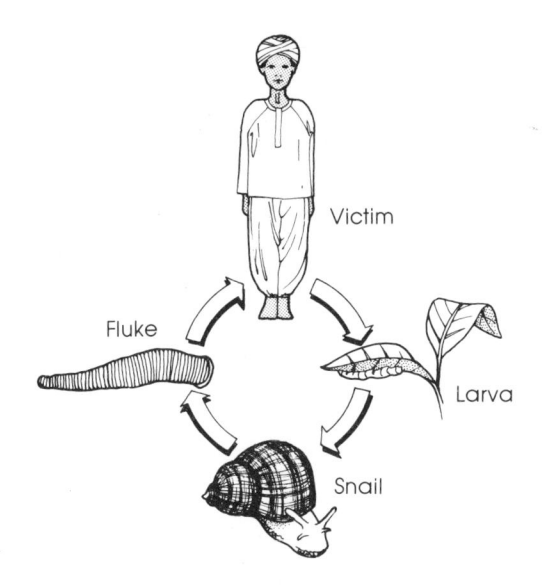

The life cycle of the bilharzia fluke

Another group of people to suffer from a side-effect of the Dam are the fishermen. The triangular area where the Nile flows into the Mediterranean is called the Delta (see the diagram overleaf). It used to be a good fishing ground. Sardines, lobster, shrimp and mackerel were caught there. Preventing the Nile silt from reaching the Delta interferes with the natural food chains. There is little plankton in the water, little for the fish to live on, and so catches are poor.

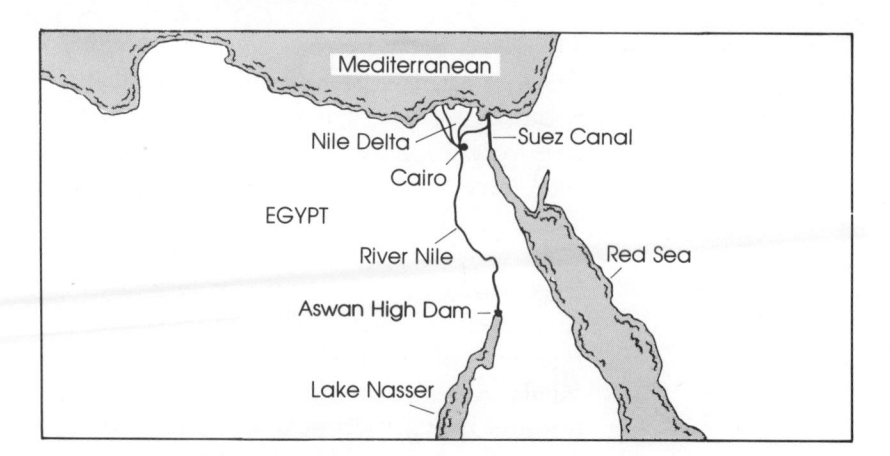

Egypt and the Nile

Was the Aswan High Dam a good investment or not? Egypt is still paying for it as she has to repay the loan from Russia. She also has to spend a lot of money on importing fertilisers. Before the Dam was built, the Nile did the job of fertilising for nothing. Lake Nasser is silting up, as the Nile silt builds up behind the Dam. The incidence of bilharzia has increased. Was it better to rely on Nature's way — flooding — to water the fields? Can science and technology be used to improve on Nature's way?

PLANTS AND WATER

When you put a plant in water, it takes in water through the roots. Plant cells are *semi-permeable*. This means that they will act as a kind of sieve, allowing water to pass through but stopping dissolved substances from passing. When a concentrated solution and a dilute solution are separated by a semi-permeable *membrane* (a thin piece of tissue, such as a cell wall) water passes from the dilute solution to the more concentrated solution. This process is called *osmosis*. Plant cells contain a dilute solution of salts. When they are placed in water, water passes into the plant cells by the process of osmosis. Water vapour passes out of the leaves in the process of *transpiration*.

ACTIVITY 6

Some experiments on plants and water

We suggest that you design experiments to answer the following questions, and then check out your ideas with your teacher.

Experiment 1

How can you find out (a) the weight of water taken up by the roots of a plant, and (b) the weight of water lost through the leaves by transpiration?

Experiment 2

What happens when you place plant material (such as strips of potato) (a) in water, and (b) in salt solution?

Experiment 3

What happens when a length of visking tubing (a semi-permeable membrane) containing sugar solution is put into a beaker of water?

Experiment 4

What makes pondweed thrive? Take pieces of pondweed in beakers to which you have added water and another substance. You could try manure, compost, fertiliser, detergent, sump oil and many other substances. Control experiments with tap-water and distilled water should be done. After 2 or 3 weeks, you will be able to see what has made the pondweed grow best.

ACTIVITY 7

Questions for discussion

This is a complex matter. We suggest that you form groups to discuss these questions. It would help you to get the feel of the arguments if you see what photographs of Egypt you can collect. Look in magazines and geography books. Photographs of the Nile and of farmworkers in the fields would help you.

1) Why did the Egyptian government decide to build the Aswan High Dam?

2) What benefit has the Dam been to farming?

3) Why do farmers now have to buy fertilisers?

4) Lake Nasser is named after a famous Egyptian. Do you know who he was?

5) How long is Lake Nasser?

6) Why is Lake Nasser gradually becoming shallower?

7) If you were a doctor treating a patient for bilharzia, what would you tell him or her to avoid on returning home?

8) If you were working for the Egyptian government, what would you do about the silt accumulating in Lake Nasser? Can you think of a use for the silt?

9) On balance, do you think the Aswan High Dam has been a benefit to Egypt?

10) Suggest what you would do to cure the problems it has created.

QUESTIONS ON WATER AND AGRICULTURE

1. Supply words to fill the blanks in this passage. Do not write on this page.

   Plants need water. They take in water through the ___ by the process of ___. This process occurs when a ___ solution is separated from a dilute solution by a ___ membrane. Water passes ___ the ___ solution ___ the dilute solution. Plants give out water through the ___ by the process of ___.

2. What has to be done to make plant cells take in water? What has to be done to make plant cells lose water? Describe an experiment which will demonstrate both of these happenings.

3. Crops need water. What do farmers do in countries with low rainfall to bring water to their crops? How did the farmers on the banks of the Nile water their fields 20 years ago, and how do they do it now? Which method do you think is better? Explain your answer.

4. Bilharzia is a disease which occurs among Egyptian farmworkers. Why has it become more common? What can a farmworker do to avoid catching the disease?

CROSSWORD ON WATER AND AGRICULTURE

First, trace this grid on to a piece of paper (or photocopy this page). Then fill in the answers. Do not write on this page.

Across

1. Floating objects ___ with the tide (5)
3. They hatch into flukes (6)
6. Has any answer been found to 21 across? (2)
7. This is how plants take in water (7)
9. It was built across 6 down (3)
11. The triangular region of 6 down (5)
14. See 4 down (3)
15. You often get this with 1 down (4)
16. A town with supposedly health-giving water (3)
18. Not me! (3)
19. Fine particles of solid in 6 down (4)
21. Most Egyptian farmworkers have this disease (9)
22. We all ___ water (4)

Down

1. This is what you get without rain or floods (7)
2. The Egyptians wanted more of this when they built 10 across (4)
3. 19 across was ___ to the farmers when the 9 across was built (4)
4, 14 across Water to the east of Egypt (3, 3)
5. Egypt's ___ was to prevent 6 down flooding (3)
6. Egypt's most important river (4)
8. South-east (2)
10. Donkey hidden by Nasser! (3)
12. The ___ content of the soils on the banks of 6 down has increased (4)
13. Where not to swim if you want to avoid 22 across (5)
16. The famous 13 down connecting 4 down, 14 across to the Mediterranean (4)
17. The name of Egypt's famous 9 across (5)
18. In a dry ___ 20 down Nasser provides a reserve of water (4)
20. Nasser is one in Egypt (4)

31

CHAPTER 3
WATER FOR WASHING

WHAT IS SOAP? HOW DOES IT WORK?

If dust falls on to clothes, it can be brushed off. If oil or grease get on to clothes, they are difficult to remove. Dust sticks to the grease, and the clothes become dirty. The problem in washing clothes is to remove oil and grease. Soaps and detergents can both do this.

A soap consists of sodium ions and soap ions. An ion is an atom or group of atoms which carries an electrical charge. A sodium ion has a positive charge, and a soap ion has a negative charge. (This should, to give it its proper name, be called a hexadecanoate ion, but we are going to call it a *soap* ion.) Each soap ion consists of two parts, a 'head' and a 'tail'. The head is water-loving, and the tail hates water but is attracted to oil and grease.

This chain of —CH_2— groups is the water-hating 'tail'

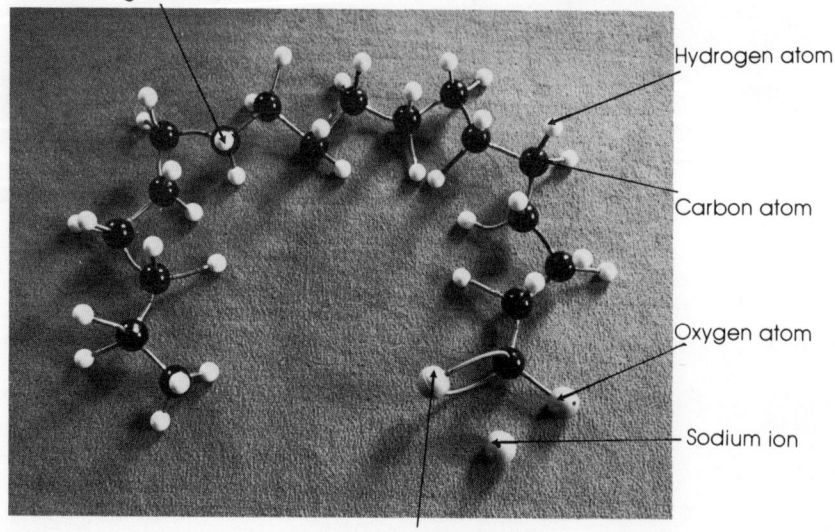

Hydrogen atom

Carbon atom

A model of the soap, sodium hexadecanoate

Oxygen atom

Sodium ion

This —CO_2^- group is the water-loving 'head'

In the next diagram, the soap ion is drawn as:

HEAD
Water-loving

TAIL
Water-hating; attracted to grease

The diagram below shows how soap ions dislodge grease from cloth. The head of each ion is attracted to the water. The tail is attracted to a grease particle. As a blob of grease becomes surrounded by soap ions, the soap ions form a bridge between the grease and the water. When they are washed, by hand or in a washing-machine, clothes are swirled around. This action dislodges the blob of grease surrounded by soap ions from the cloth, and it floats off into the water. The dirty water must be removed by rinsing. However good the soap is, if rinsing is not thorough, dirt and grease will go back on to the cloth.

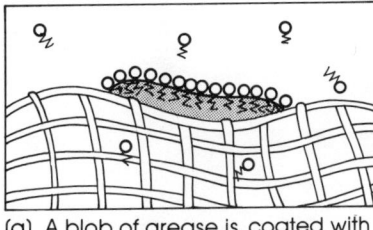

(a) A blob of grease is coated with water-hating tails of soap ions

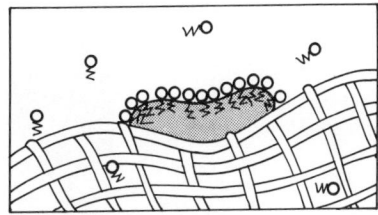

(b) The blob of grease is squeezed away from the fibre so that the water-loving heads can be surrounded by water

The action of soap on grease

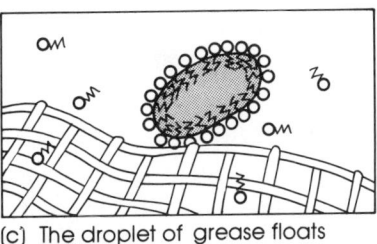

(c) The droplet of grease floats away

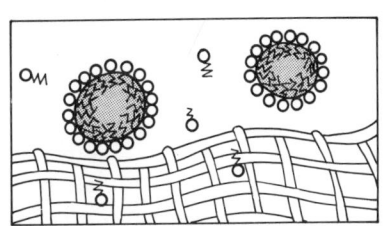

(d) Droplets of grease are prevented from touching by their coating of water-loving heads; they remain spread out through the water

Soaps are made from fats and oils. The process is called *saponification*. The fat or oil must be boiled with a strong alkali. Then salt is added to help the soap to separate out from solution.

DETERGENTS

Detergents are similar to soaps. They also have a chain of —CH$_2$— groups, which form a water-hating tail. The difference is in the water-loving head. It is a group which contains sulphur and has the formula —SO$_3^-$. Soaps and detergents are affected differently by hard water.

HARD AND SOFT WATER

We say that water is 'hard' if it is hard to obtain a lather with soap. Detergents will still lather in hard water.

Hard water (on the right), and soft water (on the left) lathering with soap

Why does hard water stop soap from lathering? The reason is that hard water contains calcium and magnesium compounds. The ions of these metals can combine with soap, and, when they do, they form insoluble compounds. We call these insoluble compounds *scum*. You have seen scum floating on top of water. Scum is not formed by detergents, You know that, if you do go on adding soap, you will eventually get a lather. This happens when there are no more calcium and magnesium ions left to form scum.

'Softening' water means removing calcium and magnesium ions. Then, soap will lather instead of forming a scum (see Activity 8, p. 36).

SOAP OR DETERGENT: WHICH IS BETTER?

Should we use soaps or detergents? Detergents pollute the water; soaps do not. Soaps and detergents are chemically similar. It is the substances called 'builders' which are added to detergents which cause the trouble. They are phosphates. They have two jobs to do. One is to make the water alkaline, which makes removal of grease easier. The other is to combine with calcium ions and magnesium ions which are present in hard water. Detergents are very powerful cleaning agents. They have the big advantage that they work in hard water.

Soaps do not work in hard water. The calcium and magnesium ions in hard water form a scum with soap. If a water-softener is used, to take out the calcium and magnesium ions, then soap will give a lather. Instead of using detergents, we could use soap and a water-softener.

People certainly seem to prefer the cleaning action of detergents to that of soaps. In 1948, detergents had 10 per cent of the cleaning market, and soaps had 90 per cent. In 1953, detergents had 50 per cent of the market. Now, the figure is 80 per cent.

There is another difficulty about abandoning detergents and going back to soap. Soap is made from vegetable oils and animal fats. The food industries also want to use vegetable oils and animal fats. Detergents are made from crude petroleum oil. The petrochemicals industry makes all kinds of things from crude oil. It makes better sense to make detergents from crude oil, and use fats and oils for food.

Perhaps you would like to try some of the experiments on the cleaning power of detergents in Activity 10, p. 37.

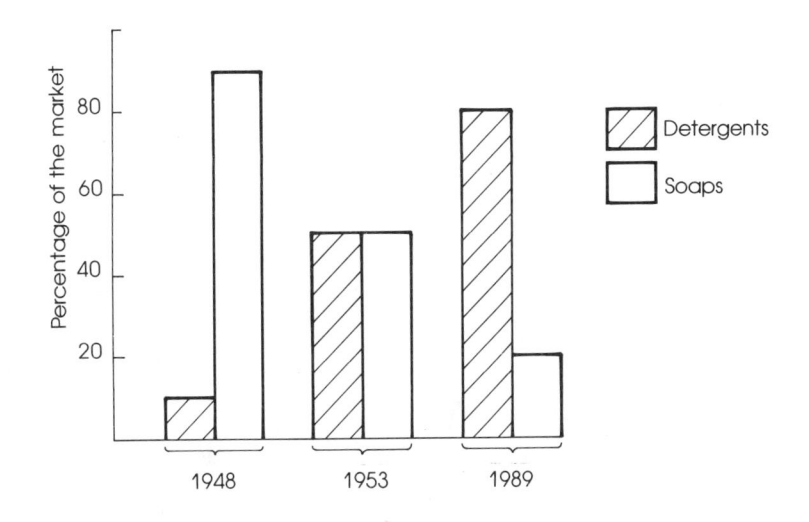

Soaps and detergents: relative sales trend

ACTIVITY 8

Construct a model water-softener

The diagram below shows one way of making a model water-softener. It uses a substance called Permutit®, which is used in domestic water-softeners. Water must be run into the top of the tube slowly. With the screw clip open, water will trickle slowly out of the tube into the beaker.

You can test the water to see how soft it is compared with the tap-water.

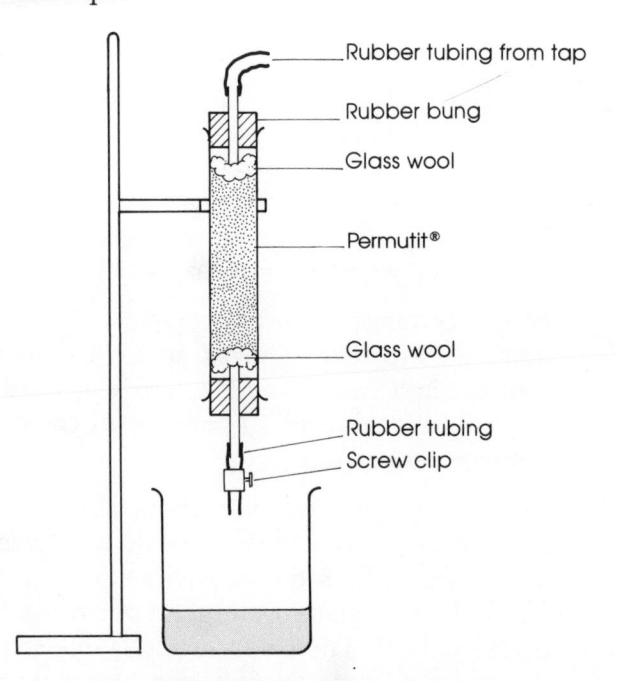

A model water-softener

The next diagram shows an experiment to find out how many drops of soap solution are needed to give a lather. You measure 25 cm³ of water. Then, you add soap solution 5 drops at a time. You must count the drops as you do so. After each 5 drops, you stopper the flask and shake it. You

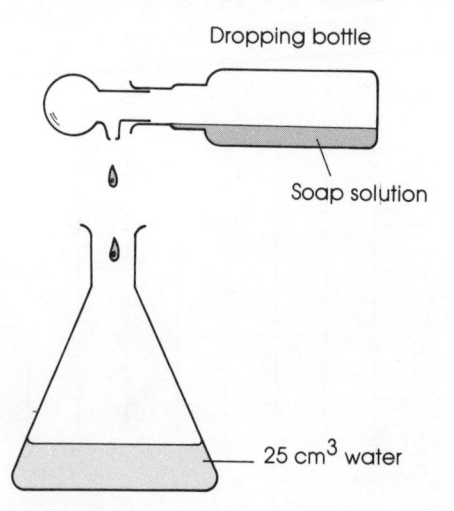

Adding soap solution

will see flakes of scum forming on top of the water. This is not lather. Lather has a frothy appearance. When a lather is formed and lasts for 30 seconds, stop adding soap solution. You have now added enough to get rid of all the hardness. Write down the number of drops of soap solution used.

It is interesting to compare results from:
- Tap-water
- Boiled tap-water
- Tap-water + a crystal of washing soda (sodium carbonate crystals)
- Distilled water
- Water from a model water-softener.

Which method gives the softest water? Is this the method you would recommend for domestic use? If not, why not? (See p. 85.)

ACTIVITY 9

Make a bar of soap

Many books give directions for soap-making.

ACTIVITY 10

Experiments on soaps and detergents

For these experiments you need:

Soap solution
Packets of: soap flakes (e.g. Lux®), non-soap detergent (e.g. Persil®), a detergent which contains soap (e.g. Fairy Soap® or Fairy Snow®), an enzyme detergent (e.g. Biological Ariel®)
Cotton rags
A selection of staining materials, e.g. tea, coffee, orange juice, blood, egg, grass, sump oil, cooking oil
Aluminium foil
Magnesium sulphate
Oven
Powdered charcoal
Universal indicator
Top-loading balance
Liquid detergent
Sodium nitrate
Calcium phosphate.

EXPERIMENT 1

Which disperses dirt better — soap or detergent?

Step 1 Put a tiny amount of powdered charcoal with 100 cm^3 of water in a conical flask. Stopper the flask, and shake well. Does the powder disperse (spread out) through the water?

Step 2 Repeat with water to which you have added one of the following:
(1) 2 cm³ soap solution
(2) 2 cm³ non-soap detergent
(3) 2 cm³ of a detergent which contains soap.

Compare your results with p. 85.

EXPERIMENT 2

Which is better at making oil mix with water — soap or detergent?

Step 1 Half fill three test-tubes with water. Into each put 1 cm³ of oil from a teat pipette.
To (1), add 2 cm³ of soap solution.
To (2), add 2 cm³ of detergent solution.
To (3), add nothing (this is the control).

Step 2 Cork each tube, shake vigorously, and allow to settle. Look at the three test-tubes. Which has emulsified the oil (made it mix with water) better — soap or detergent?

Compare your results with p. 85.

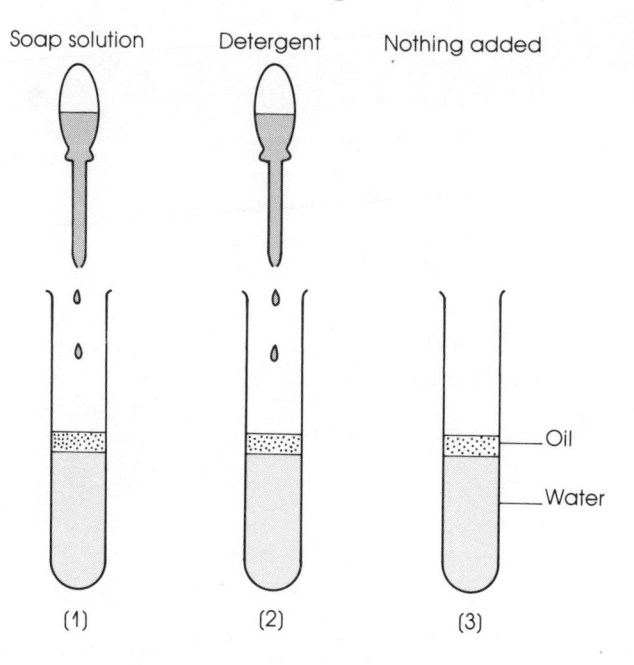

Oil and water

EXPERIMENT 3

Do soap and detergent lather in hard water?

Step 1 Number four test-tubes. Place them in a rack. Half fill them with water. To test-tubes (2) and (4), add 0.5 g of magnesium sulphate crystals. Shake until all the crystals dissolve.

Step 2 To test-tubes (1) and (2), add 1 cm^3 of soap solution. To test-tubes (3) and (4), add 1 drop of liquid detergent. Shake all the tubes. Observe which test-tubes have a lather. Does any tube have a result other than lather? Does magnesium sulphate allow soap to lather? Does it allow detergent to lather?

Compare your results with p. 85.

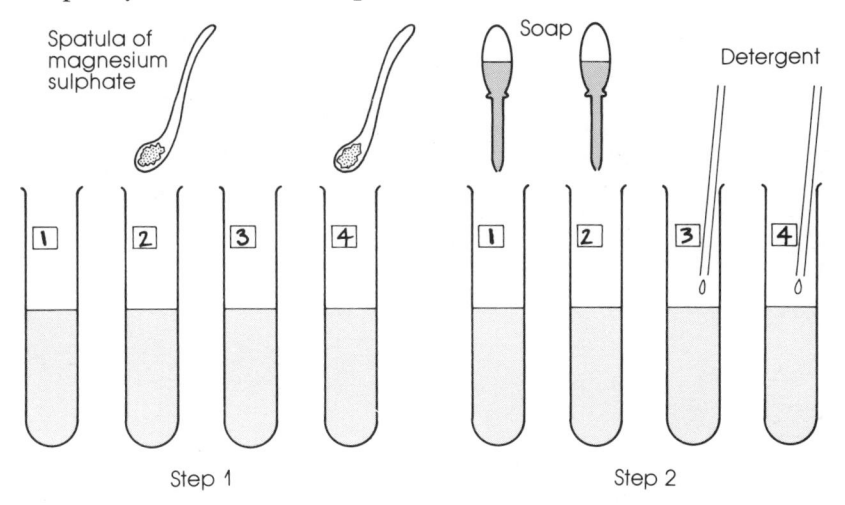

EXPERIMENT 4

Which are the most alkaline detergents?

Step 1 Make up solutions (1 g in 1 litre) of the detergents you have collected. Label the solutions.

Step 2 Take one solution in a test-tube. Add 5 drops of universal indicator. Shake the test-tube. Compare the colour with the universal indicator chart. Write down the pH number. Solutions with a pH greater than 7 are alkaline. The higher the pH, the more alkaline the solution.

Compare your results with p. 85.

Matching against the colour chart

EXPERIMENT 5

Which are better — enzyme detergents or non-enzyme detergents?

Note. An enzyme is a large protein molecule with a very special job to do. Its job is to assist a chemical reaction which takes place in a plant or animal. It might be one of the reactions which takes place when we digest our food. The enzyme speeds up the reaction.

Step 1   Take some squares of cotton rag. Stain them with different substances. You might try egg, orange juice, tea, grass, coffee and many others. Leave the stains to dry.

Step 2   Prepare 1 per cent solutions of an enzyme detergent (e.g. Biological Ariel®) and a non-enzyme detergent.

Step 3   Label a set of beakers:
   Egg + enzyme detergent
   Egg + non-enzyme detergent
and so on.

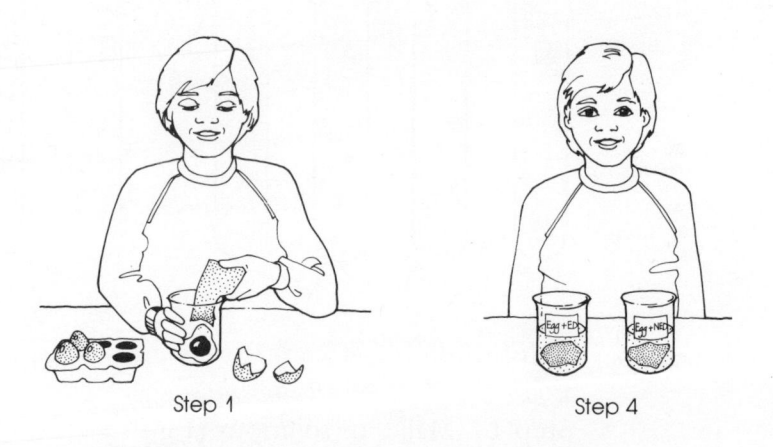

Step 1

Step 4

Step 4   Cut each square of cloth in two. Put half the egg-stained cloth into the beaker labelled 'Egg + enzyme detergent' and the other half into the beaker labelled 'Egg + non-enzyme detergent'. Add the correct detergent to the two beakers.

Deal with the other pieces of stained cloth in the same way.

Step 5   After 30 minutes, fish out the pieces of cloth. Which are cleaner — the ones soaked in enzyme detergent or the others? (See p. 85.)

Extension Work   You can extend this experiment. You found out in Experiment 4 which detergents are strongly alkaline and which are weakly alkaline. You could compare their cleaning power by the method you used in Experiment 5. You might try different detergents and different stains.

You could design an experiment to test whether the detergents work better in cold water or hot water. Again, test different stains.

You could compare the ease of washing out fresh stains and dried-on stains. Do detergents work better if the stain is fresh?

EXPERIMENT 6

Which detergent gives you the most for your money?

Note. You can see that the prices of detergents vary. It is interesting to find out whether they all contain the same amount of water. You can then compare the price with the water content. This will help you to decide which is the best buy.

Step 1 Make a small flat-bottomed tray from aluminium foil. Tear off a 10 cm square of aluminium foil. Pinch the corners together, as in the diagram. Fold the corners along the sides of the square to make a tray. Press the corners together so that the tray will hold liquid detergent.

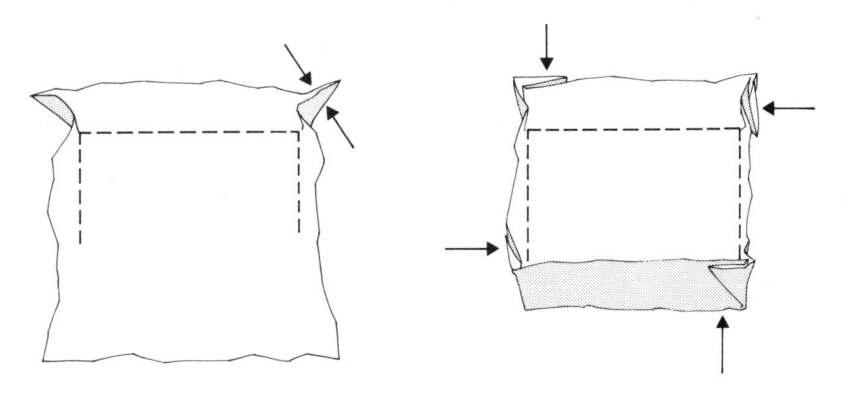

Step 2 Weigh the tray on a top-loading balance. Write down the weight. Weight = w_1 grams. Put about 5 g of detergent into the tray. Reweigh. Weight = w_2 grams.

Step 3 Put the tray into an oven at 110°C. Leave it to dry for an hour or overnight. Reweigh the tray. Weight = w_3 grams.

Step 4 Calculate the percentage of water in the sample:
Weight of sample = $w_2 - w_1$ grams
Weight of water = $w_2 - w_3$ grams

$$\text{Percentage of water} = \frac{w_2 - w_3}{w_2 - w_1} \times 100\%$$

Work out the price of each detergent per 100 g. For example, a bottle containing 500 g for 31 p costs $\frac{31}{5}$ = 6.2p per 100 g.

Step 5 Repeat the test with other detergents. Make a table of your results. Which detergent has the lowest price? Which has the lowest water content? Can you spot a 'Best Buy' which gives the most detergent for the money?

Table of Results

Detergent	Price (p per 100 g)	Percentage of Water
Whizz	6.2	20

QUESTIONS ON SOAPS AND DETERGENTS

Supply words to fill the spaces in the passages in questions 1 and 2. Do not write on this page.

1 Soaps and detergents remove ____ and ____ from cloth. Both soap and detergent ions have long chains of ____ groups. These form a 'tail' which is water-____. Soap ions and detergent ions also have a 'head' which is water-____. When clothes are washed, the heads of soap ions are attracted to ____, and the tails are attracted to ____. Thus, soap ions form a bridge between ____ and ____. This helps ____ to float off the cloth into the water. Dirty water must be removed by ____. In hard water, ____ work better than ____.

2 Soap is made from oils and fats by boiling with ____. In soft water, soap produces ____. In hard water, ____ is formed. The reason is that ions of the metals ____ and ____ are present in hard water. They combine with soap to form ____. If you go on adding soap to hard water, in the end, ____ is formed.

3 What is removed when water is softened? What crystals can be added to water to soften it? (Give the trade name and the chemical name.) What water-softener is put into columns so that water can trickle through it? Which method of softening gives the purest water? Why is this method not employed for use in the home?

4 What are algae? What is the connection between detergents and algae? Describe what happens to swimmers and boaters when algae multiply. Why is this more likely to happen in a lake than in a river?

Algae cannot go on multiplying indefinitely because they exhaust their supply of a certain substance. What is it? What happens when algae run short of this substance? Is any plant or animal other than algae affected?

5 This information comes from a packet of Biological Surf® Automatic washing powder.

Biological Surf® Automatic
NEW IMPROVED
LOW-TEMPERATURE CLEANING POWER

New Surf® Automatic has been improved to give you more active cleaning power at low temperatures.

Use new Surf® Automatic on a 40°C programme for first-rate active cleaning of the toughest dirt.

Surf® Automatic's new fragrance gives your whole wash a longer lasting freshness.

New Surf® Automatic is less harsh and therefore kinder to your clothes.

In common with other washing powders, Surf® Automatic has a biological action and contains brightening agents specially designed for safe use in washing products.

For best results in automatic machines

Use 2 cups. For tough dirt and stains use the prewash.

Handwashing or soaking

Use $\frac{1}{2}$ cup of powder. Dissolve powder thoroughly before immersing clothes.

1. Always follow the care label.
2. Never soak silk, wool, leather or garments with metal fasteners.
3. Do not use an enamel bath for soaking.
4. Flame-resistant finishes should never be soaked or washed above 50°C.
5. Any non-colour-fast fabric should not be soaked and should be washed separately in a warm solution (below 40°C).

HAND-CARE

This powder is specially formulated for automatic washing-machines. However, if you use it in the hand-wash (or for soaking) be sure to rinse your hands and dry them thoroughly. People with sensitive or damaged skin should pay particular attention to this, and should avoid prolonged contact with the washing solution.

(a) List the claims that are made for Biological Surf® Automatic.

(b) Describe the experiments you would do to test whether these claims are true.
(c) Explain what is meant by 'biological action'. What must Biological Surf® Automatic contain to have a biological action?
(d) What instructions are given for washing non-colour-fast fabrics? How could you test to see whether the method suggested is a good one?
(e) Why is it important to rinse clothes thoroughly?
(f) Explain why instructions are given for hand-care.

6 Hard water contains calcium compounds and magnesium compounds. As a result, when hard water is heated in a boiler, *scale* (which consists of calcium carbonate and magnesium carbonate) is deposited on the inside of the boiler. Scale is a poor thermal conductor. As scale builds up in the boiler, more energy is needed to heat the water. A technician found the percentage of energy wasted for different thicknesses of scale. Her results are tabulated below.

Thickness of scale (mm)	Percentage of energy wasted (%)
2	13
4	26
8	35
12	55
16	70

(a) On graph paper, plot the percentage of energy wasted (vertical axis) against the thickness of scale (horizontal axis).
(b) From the graph, say what percentage of energy is wasted when the scale is (i) 6 mm thick, (ii) 10 mm thick.
(c) From the graph, describe the way in which the percentage of energy wasted changes as scale builds up.

7 In the beginning our water is pure and soft and gentle, but underground, deep down amongst the sedimentary rocks, lurk scale and scum. They dissolve in our water and are carried through the mains water-pipes to our homes.

This is part of an advertisement for a water-softener. Explain what is wrong with the statement that scale and scum are lurking underground. How in fact are (a) scale and (b) scum produced?

CROSSWORD ON SOAPS AND DETERGENTS

First, trace this grid on to a piece of paper (or photocopy this page). Then fill in the answers. Do not write on this page.

Across

1. In ___ water, it is difficult 19 across, 14 down (4)
3. A soap should have a nice one (5)
7, 15 across Add this to soften water (7, 4)
10. See 20 across
11. A useful thing to do the washing in (7)
13. Chemical symbol for aluminium (2)
15. See 7 across
16. A new washing powder will need a ___ before it is sold to the public (5)
17. Short for saint (2)
18. Produced by soap in hard water (4)
19. (2 words), 14 down This is why you add soap (2, 3, 6)
20, 10 across This is what you must give clothes after washing with soap or detergent (8, 5)

Down

2. A way of getting very pure water (12)
4. Salts of this metal make water hard (9)
5. This substance is used in domestic water-softeners (8)
6. An old-fashioned way of warming the water is to put it on this (4)
8. Chemical symbol for nickel (2)
9. The parts of soap ions which are water-loving (5)
12. Grease helps dirt to ___ to fabrics (5)
14. See 19 across
18. You can use a ___ for adding soap powder (5)

45

CHAPTER 4

POLLUTION

POLLUTION BY INDUSTRY

Rivers

CASE HISTORY 5

The River Irwell

The Irwell rises in the Pennine Hills. It wends its way down to Manchester, where it joins the Manchester Ship Canal. This flows into the Mersey Estuary and out to the Irish Sea. A stretch of the Irwell is shown in the diagram opposite. It takes waste material from all these factories. Little wonder that in 1970 it was the most polluted river in England! Since 1970, the industries on its banks have controlled the amount of waste they discharge into it. The level of dissolved oxygen has risen, and fish and plants live in the water again.

Polluters of our rivers

However, the success story of rivers in the UK has not continued. At present, pollution is increasing at a fast rate. A *Sunday Times* team investigated the state of UK rivers early in 1989. They found that 450 miles of top-quality river had been polluted in 2 years. In 10 per cent of our rivers, fish can no longer survive. The pollution is the result of widespread defiance of the laws against pollution.

In 1988, 23 000 pollution incidents were reported. Industry was responsible for 37% of these. Water authorities, through their sewage-works, accounted for 20%; farmers accounted for 19%, and 24% were unexplained. The increase in pollution is the most dramatic since the survey began in 1958. Tens of thousands of fish have been killed, mainly by lack of oxygen.

The worst polluters are British Coal, Coal Products, ICI, Express Foods, British Tissues and the Anglian Water Authority. These six firms have had the most prosecutions for breaking pollution laws from 1983–89.

Coal Products is a subsidiary of British Coal. It makes Phurnacite®, Sunbrite® and other smokeless fuels. The filth

The River Irwell

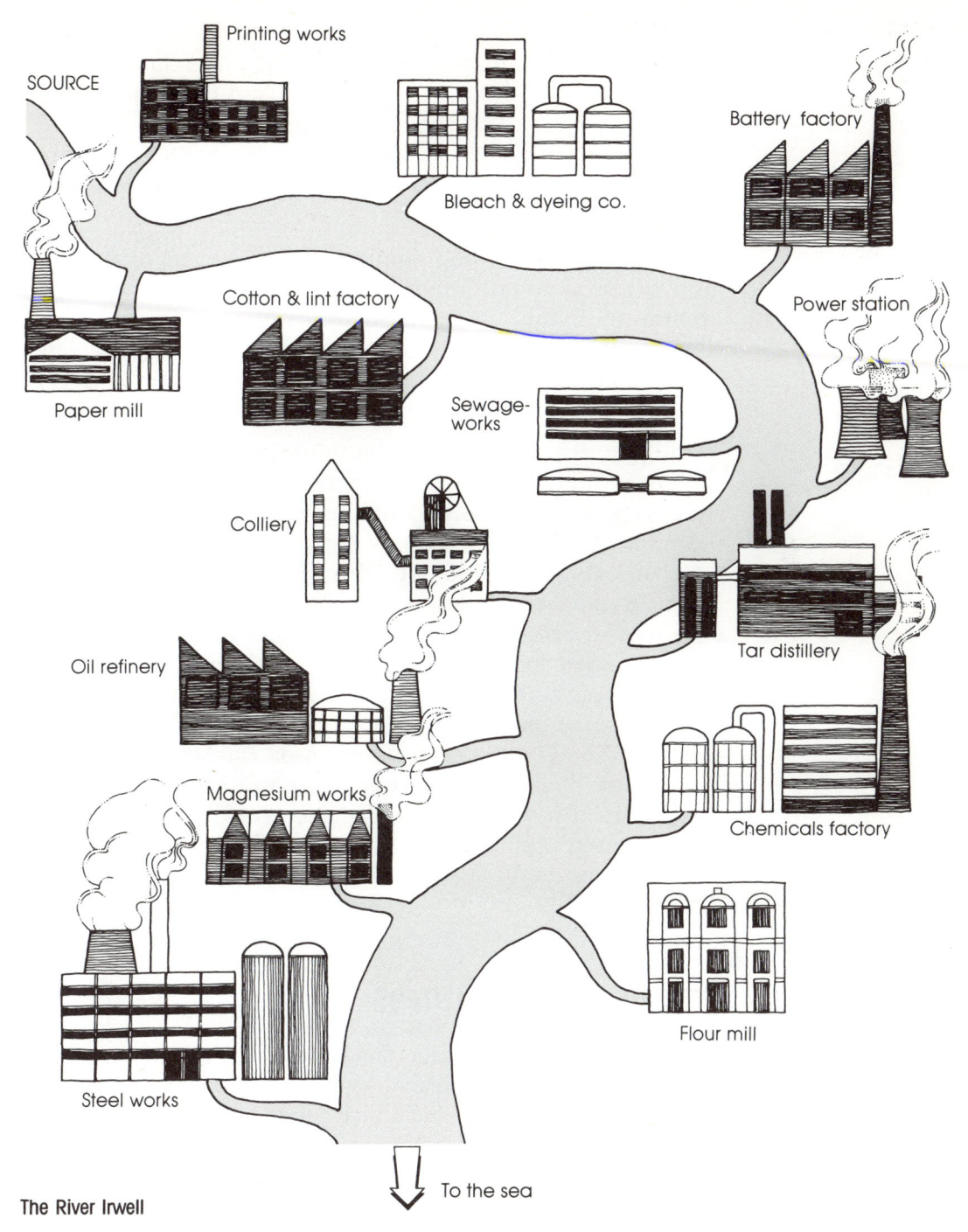

extracted from the coal in the coking process ends up in the rivers of Derbyshire and South Wales. The plant has never been prosecuted. The Phurnacite® plant in South Wales was fined £1000 in 1988 and £700 in 1989 for polluting the River Cynon. The only time the river has run clear in recent years was in 1984, when the miners' strike closed the plant. British Coal's discharges rarely meet the standards of the Welsh Water Authority.

British Tissues make toilet paper and other products. In 1986, the firm's factory in mid-Wales was fined for polluting the River Llynfi with bleach. In 1988 it polluted the same river again, and 30 000 trout and salmon were killed. The British Tissues plant near Sheffield was fined £750 in 1983. The firm continued to pollute the water. It seems as though treating the waste would cost more than paying the fines.

The Express Foods group dumps waste into some of Britain's most beautiful rivers. The group has been convicted of 25 offences in 6 years. In one incident, its plant in Cumbria allowed 100 gallons of ammonia to leak into the River Eden, killing plant and animal life over a five-mile stretch of river. The firm was fined £25 000.

In the past, the regional water authorities told industrial firms what quantities of waste materials they could discharge into rivers. The water authorities did not control the discharge of waste into tidal rivers, estuaries and the sea. The situation changed in 1989 after the UK Government passed a bill to 'privatise' the water industry. In 1989, the water authorities were sold to private companies. The water industry is run for profit, as other industries are. A new National Rivers Authority has been set up by the Government. Its job is to watch over the quality of river-water and to crack down on polluters. The Opposition spokesman on the Water Bill, Ms Ann Taylor, doubts whether our rivers will improve. She thinks that, if it was difficult to prosecute polluters when the water industry was in public hands, it will be even harder now that it is privatised.

QUESTIONS ON POLLUTERS

1. British Tissues use large quantities of bleach to turn paper white. They do this so that you can buy 'pure white' paper tissues and toilet paper.
   (a) Is the use of bleach for this purpose (i) necessary for the consumer, (ii) good for the environment?
   (b) What action could customers take to persuade British Tissues not to use large quantities of bleach?

2. Smokeless fuels are held to have advantages over coal.
   (a) How does the manufacture of smokeless fuels
      (i) reduce the pollution of air (see Extending Science 1: *Air*),
      (ii) increase the pollution of water?
   (b) Can you suggest how manufacturers of smokeless fuels can avoid polluting the water?

CASE HISTORY 6

Pollution in the Rhine

On 1 November, 1986, a fire broke out in a warehouse at the Sandoz chemicals factory near Basle in Switzerland. Firefighters sprayed the building with water, about 25 million litres (5 million gallons) of water. Due to poor planning, the tanks which were placed to collect waste-water would hold only 50 000 litres (10 000 gallons). The rest of the water overflowed and poured into the Rhine. It carried with it chemicals from the exploding drums in the burning warehouse. A slick of chemicals 80 km long began a 1200 km journey down the Rhine from Basle through West Germany and the Netherlands to the North Sea.

It was not until three days after the fire that the Swiss were able to find out which chemicals had been stored in the warehouse. They found out that 1250 tonnes of agricultural chemicals had flushed into the river. They included 900 tonnes of pesticide and 12 tonnes of organic compounds of mercury. The pesticides wiped out *micro-organisms* (microscopic plants and animals) in an 800 km stretch of the river. The fish which feed on the micro-organisms were also affected. Eels died as poisons sank to the bottom of the river where they live. Shoals of dead eels and fish had to be removed from the river. As half-dead eels washed into the North Sea, they were eaten by sea birds and mammals. The dangers of mercury compounds in the food chain are described on p. 52–3.

The map overleaf shows how pollutants from the Swiss accident flowed through West Germany and the Netherlands. Towns in West Germany had to turn off their water-intakes to prevent water from the Rhine entering their supplies of drinking-water. The Dutch had to close dams to channel the flow of the Rhine water away from reservoirs and into the North Sea. Once in the North Sea, the pollutants were forgotten.

It could take 10 years for life to return to the river. All the eels for 400 km from Basle died and micro-organisms were wiped out as far downstream as Holland. In branches of the river, some fish and plankton survived, and these may be able to recolonise the river. Before the end of the month, five more accidents in Switzerland and Germany had polluted the water and the air along the Rhine.

You will be wondering what caused the fire which started the trail of destruction. Sandoz, the chemical manufacturers, found that the fire was started by an electrical fault. This had been caused by an animal gnawing on electrical wiring in the warehouse. The firm promised to pay for all the damage it had caused.

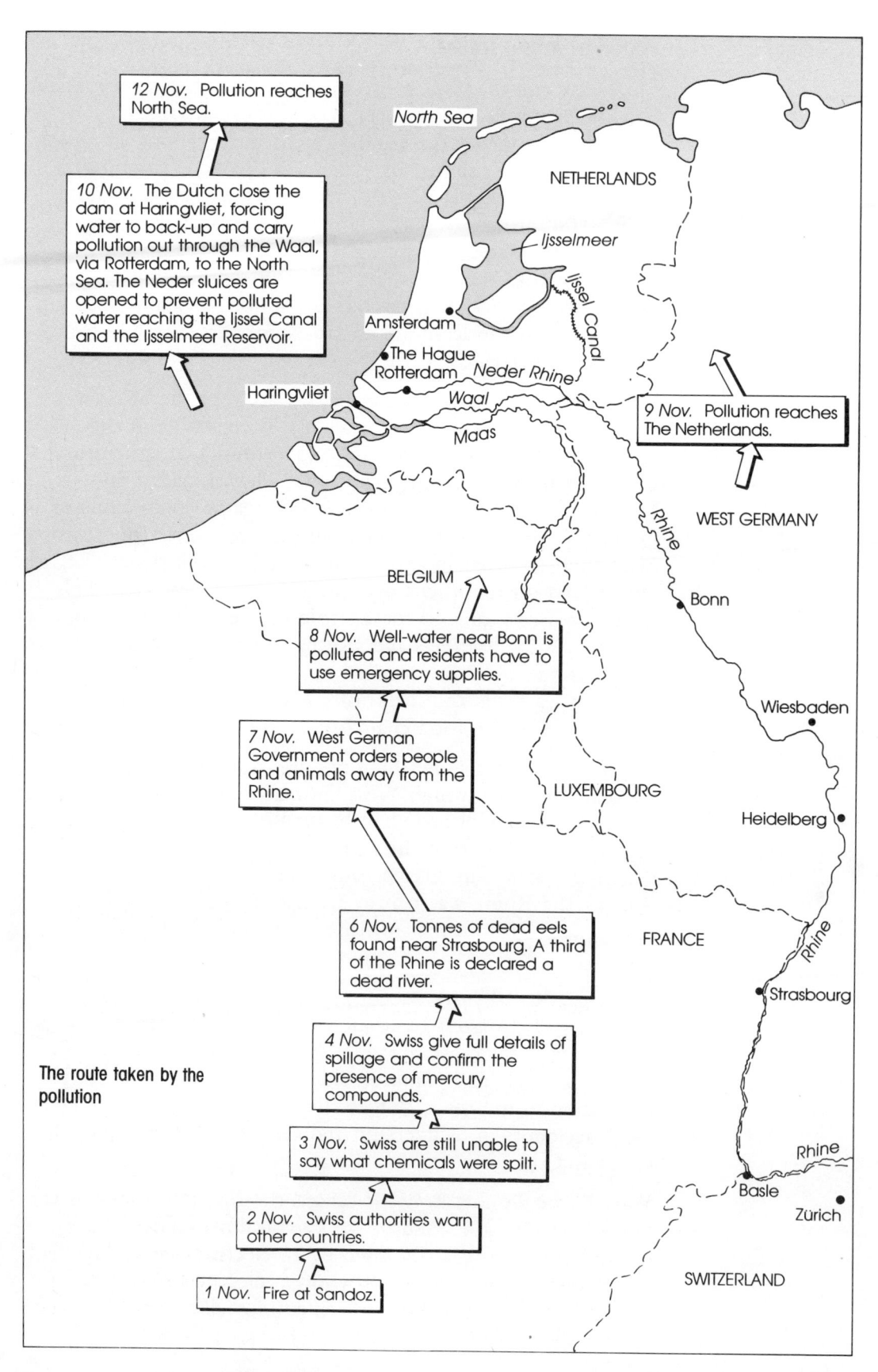

The route taken by the pollution

12 Nov. Pollution reaches North Sea.

10 Nov. The Dutch close the dam at Haringvliet, forcing water to back-up and carry pollution out through the Waal, via Rotterdam, to the North Sea. The Neder sluices are opened to prevent polluted water reaching the Ijssel Canal and the Ijsselmeer Reservoir.

9 Nov. Pollution reaches The Netherlands.

8 Nov. Well-water near Bonn is polluted and residents have to use emergency supplies.

7 Nov. West German Government orders people and animals away from the Rhine.

6 Nov. Tonnes of dead eels found near Strasbourg. A third of the Rhine is declared a dead river.

4 Nov. Swiss give full details of spillage and confirm the presence of mercury compounds.

3 Nov. Swiss are still unable to say what chemicals were spilt.

2 Nov. Swiss authorities warn other countries.

1 Nov. Fire at Sandoz.

The Swiss Government was criticised for the way it reacted to the accident. It played down the seriousness of the pollution. It was 40 hours before it warned other countries of the pollutants which were flowing towards them. The European Community (EC) called for a new alarm system to warn EC states of hazards to the environment. Switzerland is not a member of the EC.

QUESTIONS ON THE SANDOZ ACCIDENT

1 Point out two things which should have been done to improve the warehouse.

2 Once the accident had occurred, what could have been done by the Swiss to minimise the effects of the pollutants?

3 What action did the West Germans take?

4 What action did the Dutch take?

5 When the pollutants reached the North Sea, everyone heaved a sigh of relief. Can the North Sea absorb an unlimited amount of pollutants?

Estuaries

The UK Control of Pollution Act was passed in 1974. It controls the pollution of estuaries, tidal rivers and coastal areas as well as inland rivers. Many firms have obtained permission to discharge more waste into estuaries than the Act allows.

Oil refineries, chemical works, steel mills and paper mills like to be near ports. They discharge their wastes into estuaries. In the 1930s, fishermen could make a living in the Mersey. Now it is too foul to allow fish to live. Firms such as ICI, UKF fertilisers, Albright and Wilson all pour waste into the estuary. Unilever, who make soaps and detergents, put 2 tonnes of solid organic waste into the estuary every day. This explains how balls of fat come to wash up on the beach at New Brighton. There is unemployment on Merseyside and the Government does not want to make life difficult for industry in the area. The industries on the banks of the Mersey have been allowed to exceed the levels set by the Control of Pollution Act. Other estuaries, the Tees, the Tyne, the Humber and the Clyde, are also badly polluted.

Mercury

Minamata is a fishing village on the shore of Minimata Bay in Japan. To many people the name Minamata means tragedy. In 1951, a plastics factory started discharging waste into the Bay. By 1953, a thousand people in Minamata had become ill. Some were crippled and others were paralysed. Some lost their sight and others lost their mental abilities. Many died.

The food chain which led to 'Minamata disease'

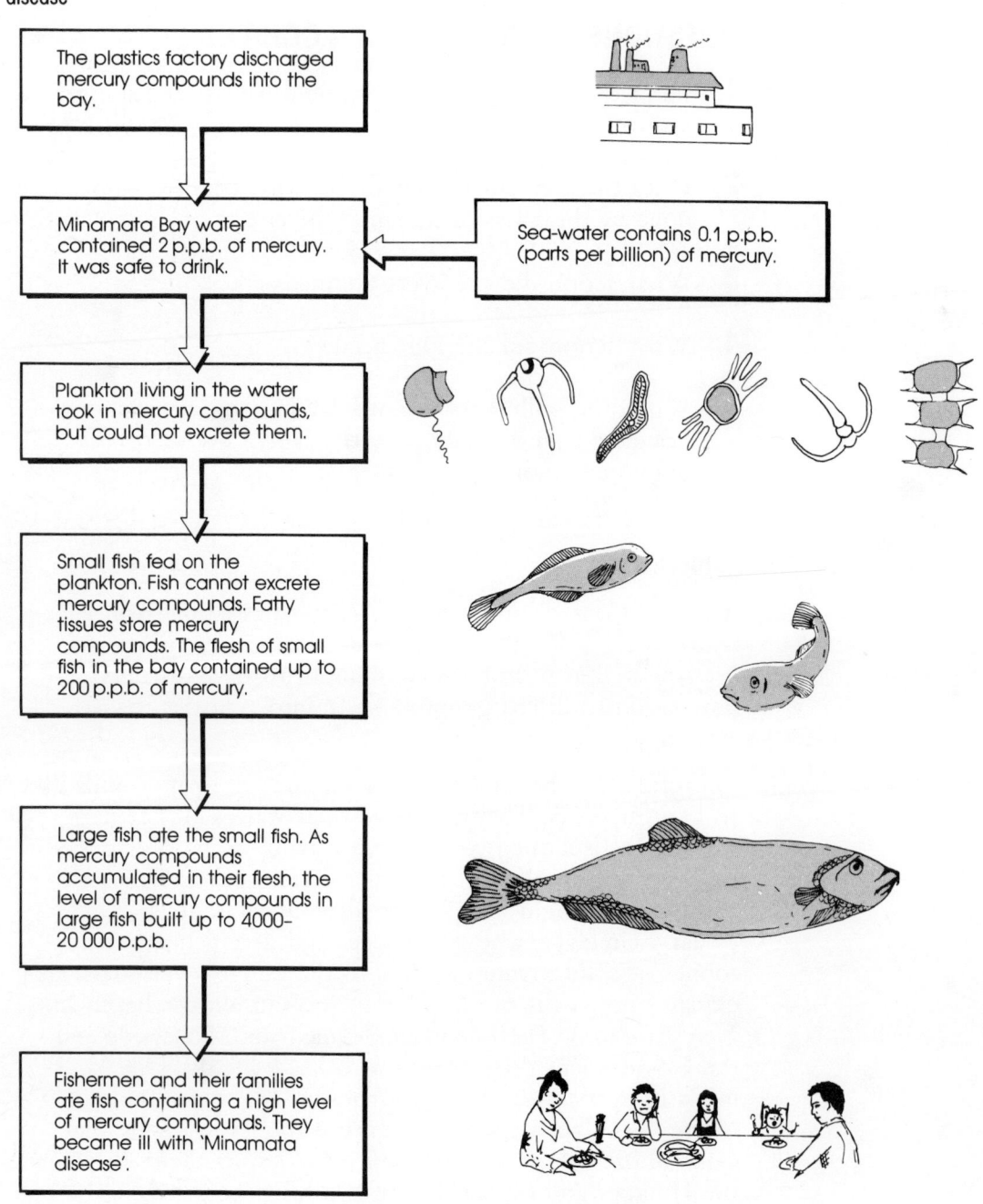

- The plastics factory discharged mercury compounds into the bay.
- Minamata Bay water contained 2 p.p.b. of mercury. It was safe to drink. ← Sea-water contains 0.1 p.p.b. (parts per billion) of mercury.
- Plankton living in the water took in mercury compounds, but could not excrete them.
- Small fish fed on the plankton. Fish cannot excrete mercury compounds. Fatty tissues store mercury compounds. The flesh of small fish in the bay contained up to 200 p.p.b. of mercury.
- Large fish ate the small fish. As mercury compounds accumulated in their flesh, the level of mercury compounds in large fish built up to 4000–20 000 p.p.b.
- Fishermen and their families ate fish containing a high level of mercury compounds. They became ill with 'Minamata disease'.

The cause of all these afflictions was traced to the mercury compounds in the waste from the plastics factory. The level of mercury compounds in the water of the bay was low, and at first scientists could not understand how it could poison people. Then they realised that the mercury compounds became part of a *food chain*. The figure opposite shows how fish in the bay came to have a high content of mercury. Fishermen and their families were poisoned by eating the fish.

In spite of Japan's experience, other countries have been slow to deal with mercury pollution. In 1967, many lakes and rivers in Sweden were found to contain dangerous levels of mercury compounds. In 1970, both Canada and the USA found that hundreds of lakes had mercury levels which made fishing dangerous. Even in 1988, ICI's plant on Merseyside discharged more mercury than the water authority permits.

POLLUTION BY SEWAGE

Most of the water that is discharged into rivers has had the full treatment. Only 85% of the sewage which is discharged into tidal waters has had the full treatment. Of the sewage that goes into the sea, 50% is untreated. Often, raw sewage is sent out to sea through long 'outfall pipes'.

Mr Nicholas Ridley, when he was Secretary of State for the Environment, defended the practice of discharging raw sewage into the sea. In the House of Commons, in March 1989, he explained that the action of salt, sunlight, water and waves broke down the sewage as well as inland sewage-treatment does. An MP for North Wales, Sir Anthony Meyer, said that there was no chance of persuading his constituents that outfalls were the best method, because sewage was often washed back on to their beaches. Mr Ridley said that outfalls should be 3–5 km long. During the debate, MPs were told that in 1989 two-thirds of British bathing beaches meet European Community (EC) standards. In 1987, only 55 per cent of the beaches met EC standards. Mr Ronald Brown, MP, asked what 'floating voters' would think of the 600 million tonnes of sewage that are poured into the seas around Britain. (This was a play on words. If you don't know, find out what a 'floating voter' is.)

The EC rules that member countries regularly test coastal regions for pollution. At each site, the coliform bacteria are counted (these bacteria can cause disease). One count is made of faecal coliforms. The number should not be more than 2000 in 100 cm^3 of sea-water. A second count is made of total coliforms. The number of these should not be more than

10 000 in 100 cm³ of sea-water. There has been little improvement in the counts over a six-year period. The table shows some results of the 1985 survey.

Coastal region	Faecal coliforms per 100 cm³ Average	Faecal coliforms per 100 cm³ Maximum	Total coliforms per 100 cm³ Average	Total coliforms per 100 cm³ Maximum
Bournemouth	50	320	100	720
Margate	115	2000	240	17 000
Poole	10	340	10	980
Ryde (Isle of Wight)	2550	80 000	5450	121 000
Sandown (Isle of Wight)	70	6100	130	7600
Southend	530	17 600	820	25 500
Weston-super-Mare	360	4300	800	13 600
Bridlington	75	590	190	700
Scarborough	305	18 800	510	18 800

QUESTIONS ON POLLUTION BY SEWAGE

1 Refer to the above table.
   (a) Name the resorts which exceeded the limit for
      (i) average faecal coliforms,
      (ii) average total coliforms.
   (b) Name the resorts which exceeded the limit for
      (i) maximum faecal coliforms,
      (ii) maximum total coliforms.
      (iii) Name any resorts which exceeded the limits on both these counts.
   (c) Friends are keen to do a lot of swimming on holiday. They ask for your advice. Using the table, list the five best resorts for your friends to visit. List the resorts in rank order.

2 (a) Explain what Mr Nicholas Ridley said to the House of Commons about natural methods of disposing of sewage.
   (b) When do natural methods become insufficient?
   (c) Why was the MP for a North Wales constituency not satisfied with discharging sewage at sea?

POLLUTION BY AGRICULTURE

Farmers and gardeners use fertilisers to increase their crop yields. Plants need the elements carbon, hydrogen, oxygen, nitrogen and phosphorus in large amounts. They can get all the hydrogen, oxygen and carbon they need from water and the carbon dioxide in the air. Nitrogen and phosphorus are more difficult to obtain. (Most plants cannot use the nitrogen in the air; see Extending Science 1: *Air*.) Fertilisers contain compounds of nitrogen and phosphorus (nitrates and phosphates). Often they are used in large quantities. Plants can absorb only a limited amount through their roots. The rest is *leached* from the soil — washed out by rain. Nitrates are very soluble; phosphates are not. Nitrates are therefore leached from the soil more quickly than phosphates are.

Rivers and lakes

The rain-water may carry dissolved fertilisers into a nearby lake or river. There the fertilisers nourish the growth of water plants. This accidental enrichment of lake-water and river-water is called *eutrophication*. It happened in Lake Erie in Canada.

CASE HISTORY 7

Lake Erie: a matter of death and life

In Canada, there is a string of enormous lakes called the Great Lakes. The map below shows where they are. Lake Ontario and Lake Erie form the border between Canada and the United States. The famous Niagara Falls lie between Lake Ontario and Lake Erie. They are one of the most beautiful sights in the world. No one could imagine, looking at them, that it would be possible to pollute such a vast quantity of water.

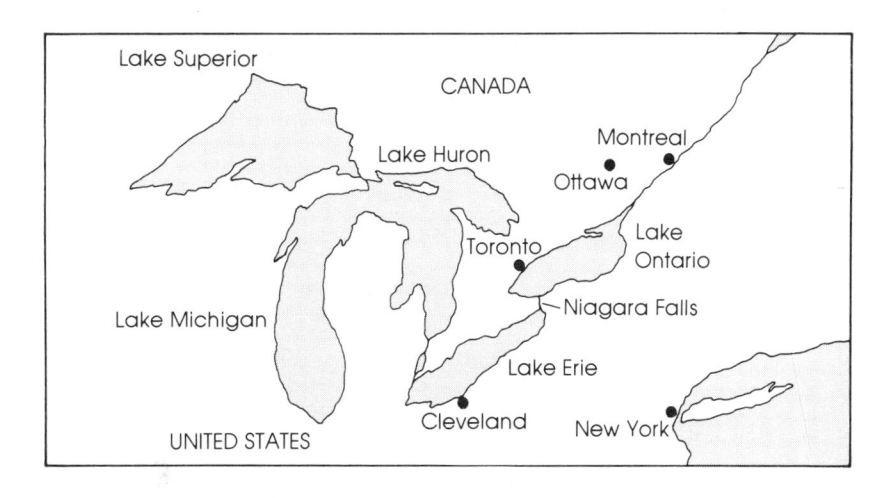

The Great Lakes

Lake Erie measures 400 km by 100 km. People like sailing on it because they can very soon get out of sight of land and enjoy a wonderful feeling of being 'away from it all'. It is not as vast as the sea, but it is much calmer for sailing. It is such a large lake that no one thought it would hurt to discharge a little sewage and factory waste into it.

They had not reckoned with the algae. Algae are the small green plant life that you see floating on small ponds. No one imagined they could take over one of the Great Lakes. Sewage entering Lake Erie contains nitrogen compounds, and algae feed on nitrogen compounds. Fertilisers washing into the Lake from the surrounding farms nourish the algae. Detergents are discharged into the Lake. They contain phosphates, on which algae thrive. The algae fed on all these waste materials being washed into the Lake. They formed a thick, green slime. Swimmers found themselves trailing ribbons of green slime. Boating became difficult as strands of algae became entangled in the propellers. Campers and picnickers no longer fancied drinking the water. Cottagers wanting to pipe water from the Lake found the filters of their water pipes became blocked with green slime.

Algae are plants. They need sunlight in order to live. When the layer of algae on the Lake became too thick, the algae at the bottom of the layer could not get any sunlight. When they die, algae are decomposed by *aerobic* bacteria (bacteria which need air). When the oxygen in the water has been used up, the aerobic bacteria die, and *anaerobic* bacteria take over. They convert part of the dead matter into smelly decay products. The rest of the debris falls to the bottom. Slowly a layer of dead plant material builds up on the bottom of the lake. With the oxygen in the water used up, fish die. Lake Erie became so bad that there were only eels and sludge worms left. This was a big disappointment to the many keen fishermen in Canada.

What can be done to bring back life to a 'dead' lake?

One answer is to bubble oxygen through it.

British Oxygen's river protection service

It is too costly for a lake the size of Lake Erie. It is done on small stretches of polluted water in the United Kingdom. The photograph opposite shows the use of oxygen to fight water pollution. A method which has been used in a smaller lake in Sweden is to pump out some of the dead and decaying matter.

These methods are very expensive, too expensive to use on a huge lake like Lake Erie. So what action did the Canadians take? They felt they could not stop the farmers using fertilisers. Instead they decided to tackle the effluent coming from Cleveland, a big industrial city on the American side of the Lake. The Americans agreed to cooperate because they too were disgusted with the state of Lake Erie. They were also in a mood to agree because of an almost unbelievable event that happened in Cleveland. One of the rivers that flow into Lake Erie caught fire! This is not an exact statement of what had happened. What really caught fire was methane gas. Methane is formed when sewage decays in water which is short of oxygen. A layer of methane on top of the water caught fire, and a bridge across the river was burned. This shocked the citizens of Cleveland, and they decided to clean up the river. As a result, the deterioration of Lake Erie has been reversed. It is now showing signs of recovery, although the fertiliser problem remains.

Many parts of the Norfolk Broads (see map overleaf) are now covered in algal bloom. Water plants have gone, killed off by competition with the masses of algae. The tourist industry centred on the Broads would like to see them restored to their former condition.

Lough Neagh in Northern Ireland (see map overleaf) is the biggest lake in the UK. It supplies Belfast with drinking-water. Algae now flourish in the lough. They block the filters through which water flows to the water-treatment plant. The lough is used for eel-fishing, but eels and other fish are now in danger. They could run short of oxygen as decaying algae use up the oxygen dissolved in the water.

ACTIVITY 11

What makes algae grow?

Step 1   Obtain some pond water with algae floating in it.

Step 2   Half fill seven beakers with the pond water. Add to each of the beakers one of the following, labelling each beaker as you do so:

(1) 1 g detergent
(2) 10 g detergent
(3) 1 g sodium nitrate
(4) 10 g sodium nitrate
(5) 1 g calcium phosphate
(6) 10 g calcium phosphate
(7) nothing.

Step 3 Stand the beakers in a light place. After 2 weeks, some beakers will show a thick growth of algae.

Extension Work Can you think out a way of weighing the amount of algae formed in each beaker?

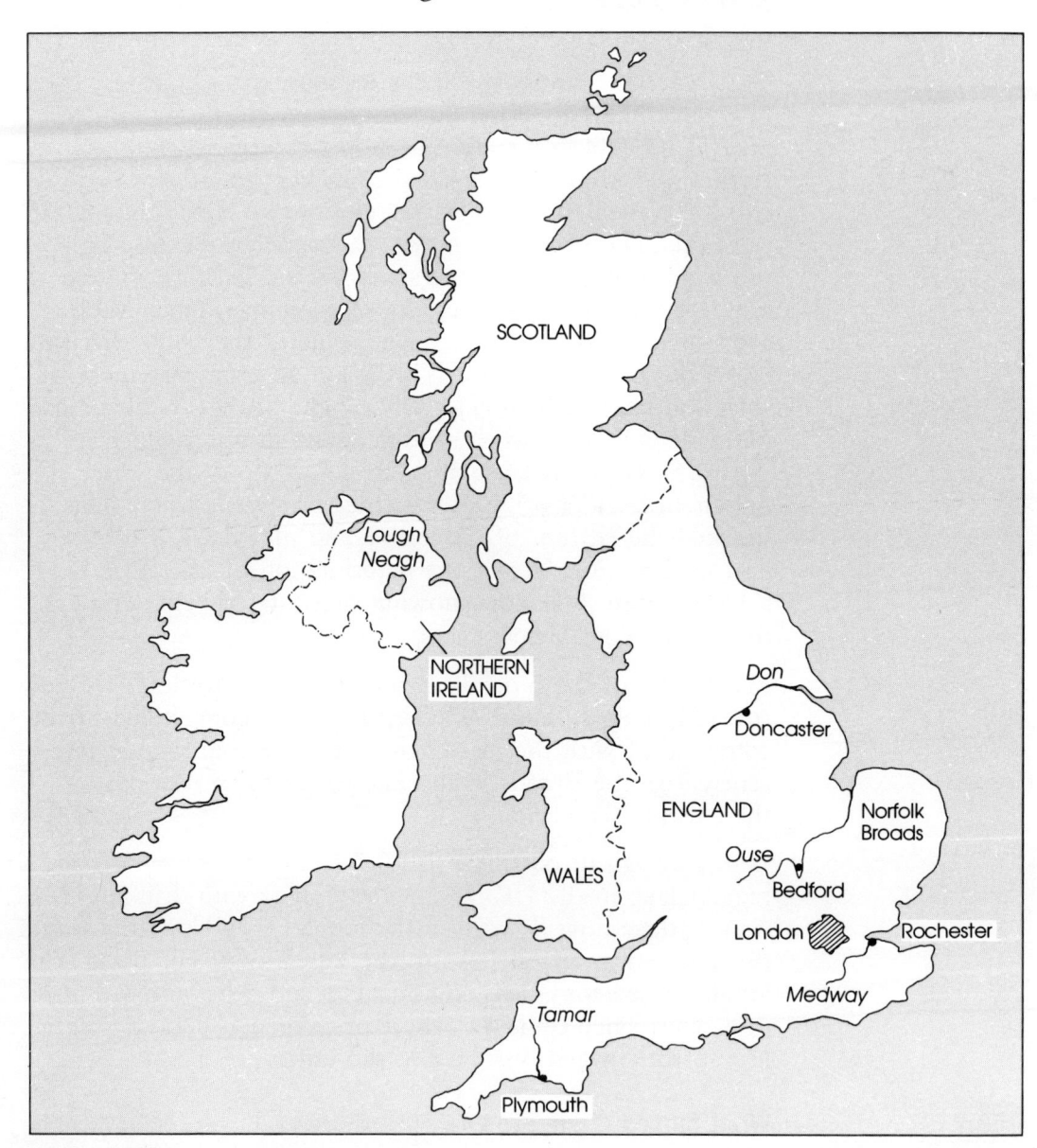

Locations of Norfolk Broads and Lough Neagh

Ground-water

Some rain-water does not find its way into lakes or rivers. It trickles down through the soil and through layers of porous rock until it meets a layer of rock which it cannot penetrate. There it stays as *ground-water*. Ground-water is held in layers of porous rock. It contains salts which have dissolved from the rocks into the water. It may also contain dissolved fertilisers. One-third of the UK's drinking-water comes from ground-water. The level of nitrate in the ground-water is rising.

By 1987, something had to be done about the UK's drinking-water. The European Community regulation is that water should not contain more than 50 mg of nitrate per litre. EC scientists found 54 sites in the UK where drinking-water exceeded this limit. (The UK had been interpreting the EC regulations loosely. The UK said that supplies could exceed 50 mg/litre of nitrate as long as the *average* level of nitrate over a three-month period did not exceed 50 mg/litre.) In 1990, the UK will be prosecuted by the EC. At least a million people are being regularly supplied with polluted drinking-water. Friends of the Earth calculate that more than 5 million people receive water that goes over 50 mg/litre of nitrate at some time. The worst areas are the east coast of England and South-East England. Eastern regions of the country have the lowest rainfall and the most intensive farming, so the accumulation of nitrate is worst there. The UK has agreed to work towards EC standards. For one water authority, a treatment plant to remove nitrate would cost about £40 million.

There are two reasons why people worry about the level of nitrate in drinking-water.

1) Nitrates are converted into compounds which oxidise haemoglobin in the blood. Oxidised haemoglobin can no longer carry oxygen round the body. Babies are more at risk than adults. In the 'blue baby syndrome', the baby turns blue from lack of oxygen. This illness is extremely rare.

2) Some scientists think that high levels of nitrates in drinking-water may lead to an increase in stomach cancer.

Farmers use about five times as much fertiliser as they did 30 years ago. Farmers may have to face controls on the amounts of fertiliser they use. The Government has considered a tax on farmers using fertiliser in the most polluted areas. The proceeds would go towards the £200 million needed to clean up the rivers and water supplies. The nitrate pollution of water supplies would continue for 15–20 years even if the use of fertilisers were stopped.

There are methods of taking nitrate out of water.

1) Chemical methods involve making the water flow through an *ion exchanger*. The ion exchanger is a column containing a chemical which takes the nitrate ion out of water and replaces it with chloride ion. Such methods produce water

which is rather salty in taste and has a high chloride content.

2) Biological methods use bacteria to feed on the nitrate. Such methods have a risk of contaminating the water with bacteria or with the methanol that the bacteria are fed with.

3) New methods combine chemical and biological techniques. Dutch research workers have developed an ion exchanger which extracts nitrate ions and replaces them with hydrogencarbonate ions. The hydrogencarbonate ions are produced by bacteria as they feed on methanol. In a second column, the nitrate ion removed by the first column is consumed by the same bacteria and turned into gaseous nitrogen. The ground-water never comes into direct contact with the bacteria. In this way, the risk of contamination is avoided. The end product is water that is free of nitrate and has a harmless hydrogencarbonate content. Bottled mineral waters contain hydrogen-carbonates. The technique is expensive: a £100 000 apparatus is needed to purify 75 m^3 (15 000 gallons) per hour. It would raise the cost of drinking-water by 2 p per m^3 (1 p per 100 gallons).

Private water companies will be paying to remove nitrate ions from the water. Farmers are adding nitrate to the soil to increase their yields — and their profits. People have suggested either taxing farmers on the amount of fertiliser they use or rationing fertiliser. The Fertiliser Manufacturers Association says that neither suggestion is the best way to control the problem. The Association calls for better farming practices as the solution. They warn that not using fertilisers will raise food prices. Agricultural advisers have drawn up a code of good farming practice. Many farmers are following the code. The main points are the following.

1) Do not apply nitrogen fertiliser in autumn.

2) Do not leave soil bare during the winter.

3) Sow winter crops in early autumn.

4) If a spring crop is to be grown, sow a fast-growing crop to cover the ground during the winter.

5) Do not plough up a large area of grassland in any one area at one time.

6) Plough in straw. (This locks up some nitrate.)

7) Use nitrogen fertiliser strictly in accordance with professional advice. Apply it only when the crop is growing actively.

QUESTIONS ON POLLUTION BY FERTILISERS

1. See whether you can explain the reasons behind the seven points in the good farming code opposite. Explain how following these seven points will reduce the amount of nitrate washed out of the soil by rain.

2. The table below shows the effect of applying nitrogen fertiliser to a field of grass.

Nitrogen fertiliser (kg/hectare)	0	100	200	300	400	500	600	700
Grass crop (tonne/hectare)	8.0	11.0	13.5	15.5	17.5	19.0	19.7	20.0

(a) On graph paper, plot the yield of grass per hectare against the mass of fertiliser per hectare.

(b) A farmer decides to apply an extra 100 kg/hectare of nitrogen fertiliser. How much does the yield of grass increase if the previous application of fertiliser was
  (i) 200 kg/hectare,
  (ii) 400 kg/hectare,
  (iii) 600 kg/hectare?

Pesticides

Farmers use fertilisers to increase their crops, and pesticides to protect them. Some pesticides are *herbicides* which destroy weeds. Others are *insecticides*, which destroy the insects that would naturally prey on crops. Rain-water washes pesticides into ground-water, just as it does with fertilisers. The pesticides dieldrin, endrin and aldrin are sometimes called the 'drins'. They cause liver damage and affect the central nervous system.

The European Community sets a limit of 5×10^{-9} g/litre (5 g per 1000 million litres) for 'drins'. Half the water in the UK exceeds this level. During the 1987 election campaign, the Government agreed to reduce the combined level of these three 'drins' to 30×10^{-9} g/litre by January, 1989. This is still far above the EC level. The danger is that fish will take in 'drins'. They are stored in fatty tissues and not excreted. Animals or humans eating fish would be eating food containing a high level of 'drins'. Pesticides are especially serious when they become part of a food chain.

QUESTIONS ON POLLUTION BY AGRICULTURE

1 The table below shows the yields of barley and potatoes for different applications of phosphate fertiliser.

Phosphate fertiliser (kg/hectare)	0	14	28	56
Yield of barley (tonne/hectare)	2.0	2.7	3.0	3.5
Yield of potatoes (tonnes/hectare)	13	29	32	32

(a) Plot the yield of (i) barley and (ii) potatoes against the quantity of fertiliser applied.

(b) Comment on the difference in shape between the two graphs.

(c) According to graph (ii), what application of fertiliser should be used on potatoes?

2 The label on a bottle of mineral water (price 42 p/litre) reads:

Carbonated
BRECON CARREG
Natural Mineral Water

Typical Analysis	mg/litre		mg/litre
Calcium (Ca)	47.5	Sulphates (SO_4)	9
Magnesium (Mg)	16.5	Nitrates (NO_3)	2.2
Sodium (Na)	5.7	Hydrogencarbonates (HCO_3)	206
Potassium (K)	0.4	Silica (SiO_2)	5.1
Chloride (Cl)	13	Dry residue at 180 °C	198

A pure natural mineral water with a consistently low salt content. This pure natural mineral water from the Brecon Carreg spring is bottled and carbonated at its source in the Brecon Beacons National Park — over four hundred square miles of scenic beauty environmentally protected by Act of Parliament. Naturally free from all forms of pollution, doesn't it make sense to enjoy this refreshing natural mineral water that lives up to its reputation as pure, fresh and natural?

Brecon Carreg natural mineral water is at its best when served chilled.

(a) (i) What does 'carbonated' mean?
(ii) Why does the firm carbonate the water before selling it?
(iii) Why is it recommended that the water is served chilled?

(b) Where do the other substances in Brecon Carreg water come from?

(c) Which metal is most abundant in Brecon Carreg water? This metal is also present in tap-water. Why is it important that drinking-water should contain salts of this metal?

(d) If you drank one litre of Brecon Carreg water, what mass of metals would you take in?

(e) From the analysis, would you expect Brecon Carreg water to be acidic, alkaline or neutral? Explain your answer.

(f) State one advantage of Brecon Carreg water over tap-water.

(g) Tap-water costs about 0.1 p per litre. How many times more expensive is Brecon Carreg water? Do you think it is worth the difference?

3 (a) State two illnesses which can be caused by too much nitrate in the drinking-water.

(b) What is the maximum level of nitrate that the European Community says should be present in drinking-water?

(c) Why has the concentration of nitrate in drinking-water increased in recent years?

(d) What do you think should be done about the problem? Some suggestions are:
- Ration fertilisers to farmers.
- Tax fertilisers.
- Stop the use of fertilisers in badly polluted areas.
- Let water authorities spend money (taxpayers' money) on methods of removing nitrates from drinking-water.
- Spend money on research into new methods of removing nitrates from drinking-water.

This is a big problem. The Government has not yet decided how to tackle it. Perhaps you should form a group to pool ideas. Then write to your MP to tell him or her what you think should be done.

WATER PRIVATISATION

The UK water supply used to be in the hands of the regional water authorities. In 1989, the Government 'privatised' water; that is, sold each of the water authorities to privately owned companies. There was much debate over these plans.

Many people think that something as important as our water supply should come under Government control, and should not be run for private profit. Will private water companies put a clean water supply and concern for the environment first? Will they be tempted to sacrifice high standards for high profits? Other people point to inefficiency in various water authorities. They point out that in many regions drinking-water is below European Community standards. They point out that sewage-treatment plants are not large enough for the needs of some areas. They say that private companies will have to be more efficient than the water authorities were in the past.

Until the 1950s, lead water-pipes were widely used in the UK. Lead is an unreactive metal, but it dissolves very slowly in water. Lead and its compounds are poisonous. Copper has replaced lead for use in water-pipes. In cold-water systems, plastic pipes are used. In hard-water areas, there is less danger from lead pipes. A layer of insoluble lead carbonate builds up on the inside of pipes. It acts as a barrier to stop more lead dissolving. In soft-water areas, the water is likely to be more acidic, and lead dissolves more quickly. Water companies make the water slightly alkaline by adding calcium hydroxide. During the 1983 strike by UK water workers, the treatment of water supplies with calcium hydroxide stopped. The level of lead in the tap-water of some houses with lead pipes rose from 40 μg/litre to 800 μg/litre. In the North-West Water Authority, 600 000 houses have lead pipes. With the water industry 'privatised', the problem of replacing old lead pipes passes from the water authorities to the new private water companies.

In many parts of the country, the sewers are very old, and parts of the sewers collapse. In some regions, the sewers are not big enough. They overflow into rivers when it rains heavily. The solution to the problem is massive expenditure on new sewers. This is difficult when the Government has reduced spending by water authorities in recent years. Private water companies have to take on the problem of Britain's ageing sewers now that the Water Privatisation Bill of 1988 has become law.

What do you think?

Should water have been privatised? This is a difficult question. Perhaps you would like to organise a debate. The table lists some of the 'pros and cons' to help you. After you have debated the matter, take a vote.

Privately owned water companies	*Publicly owned water authorities*
The cost of water is expected to rise.	The price of water was low.
It is not clear whether there will be workable arrangements for the control of pollution.	The Government had control over pollution. Nevertheless, many of our rivers are polluted.
Private companies will be more sensitive to pressure from the public. It will be easier for the customer to insist on improvements.	Most water authorities held their meetings in secret. They gave out very little information to the public.
Private companies will have to take notice of what their shareholders want.	Very few polluters were prosecuted. When they were, fines were small.
The cost of using rivers for fishing and boating is expected to rise.	Fishing, boating and other leisure activities were low-cost.
Foreign countries can buy up our water companies.	Many people think our water supply should be kept in British hands.
Private water companies are expected to sell off land on river banks and other scenic areas for development.	Land bordering river banks is strictly reserved. It is home to many animals and plants. River banks are used for leisure activities.
Regional water authorities have not replaced all the old lead pipes and defective sewers. To do so will cost a lot of money.	Public water authorities were not run for profit. Their profits could be used to improve the service.
Private water companies may not continue to add fluoride.	Regional water authorities added fluoride to water supplies.

QUESTIONS ON WATER QUALITY

1 Water authorities set limits for the quantities of wastes which industries are allowed to discharge into rivers. They had difficulty in making industrial firms keep to these limits. Will private water companies be able to do better?

2 The table shows data on river-water quality. (The map on p. 58 shows where the rivers are.) The figures are taken from data produced by the Department of the Environment, 1987.

Anglian Water Authority
River Bedford Ouse

Year	pH	Dissolved oxygen (mg/litre)	Biochemical oxygen demand (mg/litre)	Nitrate (mg/litre)
1976	8.3	10.10	5.6	8.86
1977	8.0	9.46	3.1	11.34
1978	8.1	9.77	3.1	10.04
1979	8.1	9.53	3.5	10.35
1980	8.3	10.44	4.4	8.40
1981	8.2	10.05	3.5	9.06
1982	8.1	10.45	—	9.52
1983	8.1	10.55	—	9.49
1984	8.2	10.96	4.2	9.64
1985	8.1	11.05	3.8	9.15

South-West Water Authority
River Tamar

Year	pH	Dissolved oxygen (mg/litre)	Biochemical oxygen demand (mg/litre)	Nitrate (mg/litre)
1976	7.7	10.79	2.3	2.53
1977	7.4	10.75	2.3	2.69
1978	7.3	10.95	2.1	2.67
1979	7.3	10.81	2.4	2.57
1980	7.2	11.10	2.2	2.49
1981	7.2	10.83	2.3	2.36
1982	6.9	10.69	2.4	2.58
1983	7.4	10.44	2.5	2.99
1984	7.4	10.01	2.7	2.95
1985	7.2	10.43	2.8	2.98

(a) Calculate the average pH between 1976 and 1985 in (i) the Ouse, (ii) the Tamar.

(b) Which water is the nearer to neutral? Suggest what might have caused the difference.

(c) Calculate the average dissolved oxygen concentration for (i) the Ouse, (ii) the Tamar.
  (iii) Calculate the difference between the two figures. Express the difference as a percentage of the larger figure.

(d) Calculate the average biochemical demand for
   (i) the Ouse (ii) the Tamar.
   (For *biochemical oxygen demand*, see p. 15.)
   (iii) Calculate the difference between the averages for the two rivers. Express the difference as a percentage of the higher of the two figures.
   (iv) Suggest a reason for the difference between the figures for biochemical oxygen demand in the two rivers.
   (v) Suggest a reason why the difference in biochemical oxygen demand is greater than the difference in dissolved oxygen concentration.
(e) Plot a graph of nitrate concentration against the year for (i) the Ouse, (ii) the Tamar.
   (iii) Describe the shape of each graph, saying whether there has been an increase or a decrease in nitrate concentration over the years.
(f) Calculate the average values of nitrate concentration for (i) the Ouse, (ii) the Tamar.
   (iii) Calculate the difference between the two values.
   (iv) Suggest why there is a big difference between them.

3 Measurements of biochemical oxygen demand in two rivers are shown in the table. (The map on p. 58 shows where the rivers are.)

River	Year	BOD (mg/litre)
Don	1976	7.1
Don	1978	4.6
Medway	1978	3.6
Medway	1980	5.2
Medway	1982	3.8
Medway	1985	2.9

(a) In 1978, which was the less polluted river, the Don or the Medway?
(b) Did the River Don improve or worsen between 1976 and 1978?
(c) Describe what happened to the quality of the water in the River Medway between 1978 and 1985.

CHAPTER 5

THE BOUNDLESS SEA

CASE HISTORY 8

A drop in the ocean

The seas are so vast that we have assumed that they will absorb all the rubbish we dump in them. In recent years, there have been more and more accidents involving oil spillage at sea. The sea has not been able to cope with it all. Accidents at oil rigs in the sea and at oil terminals, where tankers load and unload, may discharge oil into the sea. Some oil tankers flush out their oil tanks at sea. This is illegal: they should do this in dock while delivering their oil. To do it at sea saves time, but it is a dreadful act of vandalism as it pollutes a vast area of sea.

Some of the oil evaporates, some dissolves, but most of it floats on the surface of the sea. Slowly, air oxidises it to carbon dioxide and water. Slowly, bacteria decompose it. But oil remains for a long time, and can do a lot of damage.

The *Torrey Canyon*

The first time the United Kingdom had to deal with a huge oil slick was in 1967. The oil tanker *Torrey Canyon* sank out at sea, off the coast of Cornwall. Eighty million litres of oil started flowing towards the coast. Detergent was sprayed on to the oil slick in huge amounts. Unfortunately, this proved not to be the best way of dealing with the problem. The oil slick spread further over the surface and affected even more seabirds and fish. The detergent proved poisonous to many creatures too. People refer to it as 'the *Torrey Canyon* disaster'. Thousands of seabirds were killed.

There was an accident involving an oil tanker called the *Amoco Cadiz* off the coast of France in 1978. Miles and miles of the beautiful beaches of Brittany were spoiled by thick oil washing in from the sea. Brittany is normally a very popular holiday area, but people gave it a miss that year. It lost money from the tourist trade. The fishermen had a bad year too as their catches were low.

Oil from the *Torrey Canyon* on a Cornish beach

What can be done?

First, what can be done to prevent oil spillage at sea? France has 'spotter' planes, which fly over the English Channel and watch out for cargo ships discharging oil into the sea. They take photographs of any ship breaking the law. France also has fast boats patrolling the Channel. They can make contact with any ship which is causing contamination. Some captains, sailing far from their own countries, are not as worried as

A cormorant covered with oil from the *Torrey Canyon*

they should be about polluting the sea. If they know there is a chance of their being spotted by a plane or boat, they are less likely to break regulations. A fine is imposed on any company whose ships break international law.

Five million litres of oil pass through the Channel each day, yet the United Kingdom has no spotter planes or patrol boats. Should we keep a closer watch on the Channel?

An Esso tanker

Secondly, what can be done about accidental spillage of oil at sea? A good example was set by San Francisco in 1971. Two tankers collided in thick fog under the Golden Gate Bridge. Three million litres of oil spilled into San Francisco Bay. Fortunately, after the oil had flowed 4 miles into the Bay, the tide turned, and the oil ebbed out. But when the tide turned again, it brought the oil flooding back along the Pacific coastline. It trapped tens of thousands of birds which winter on the shores of San Francisco Bay.

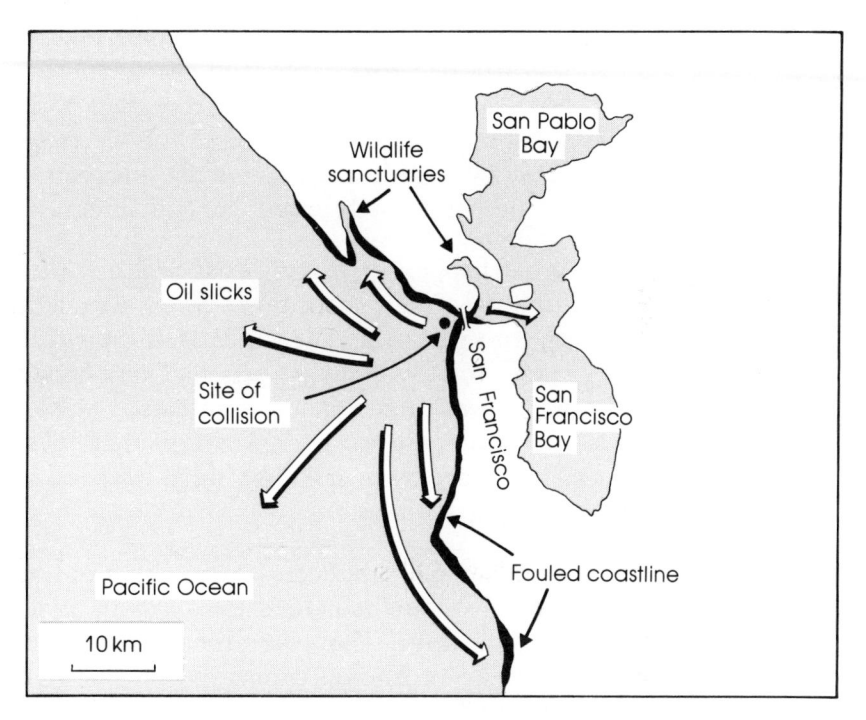

San Francisco Bay

The Standard Oil Corporation accepted responsibility for dealing with the damage their tankers had caused. They did not rush in with detergent, because the *Torrey Canyon* disaster in 1967 had shown that this was not the best remedy. They rushed 40 000 bales of straw to the coast, which may seem a strange way to deal with oil. The straw was dropped into the sea by helicopter, from barges and boats, and pushed into the sea by volunteers working on the shore. Straw is able to soak up from 5 to 40 times its own weight of oil. When soaked with oil, the straw had to be picked up again from the sea. Some of it was picked up by people going out in boats with pitchforks — 2000 pitchforks went into use. Thousands of volunteers stood on the beaches, picking up the bales of sodden straw as they washed ashore. The straw was loaded on to trucks and driven away to be dumped in pits. For three days, volunteers and oil company employees worked around the clock to protect the coastline. The map above shows how the oil spread and where fouling of the beaches occurred.

Standard Oil spent £2 million on cleaning up. They sucked up a large amount of oil from the sea with vacuum pumps. Tanker lorries were driven on to barges, and floated out to sea. Pumps sucked oil from the sea into the tanks. Then the lorries were driven to refineries where the oil was reclaimed.

Another technique was to make floating barriers. Volunteers made a floating barrier to keep the oil from entering Bolinas Lagoon, a sanctuary for seabirds.

A clever idea was to make a line of floating booms. One end was attached to a barge, and the other to a small boat. The boat set off from the barge and made a circle round bales of sodden straw. Then it headed for the barge, towing the bales of straw with it as shown in the diagram opposite. The crew of the barge pitchforked the sodden straw aboard.

What happened to the birds? Seabirds sit on the sea and dive for food. These poor birds dived into clean water and came up into thick oil. The oil matted their feathers, and they could not fly. Many drowned. Their insulation from the cold water was ruined. They were tossed helplessly to and fro on the water, and many died before they reached the shore. Those that were still alive were wrapped up and taken to cleaning stations.

Standard Oil supplied 100 000 litres of mineral oil to clean them. Volunteers bathed the birds in mineral oil and dried them in flour. They were then cared for until they could swim again. The oil company paid out £500 a day for food and medicines. In spite of all this care, only a very small fraction of the birds survived. You may be interested in Activity 12, p. 80, which is about removing oil from feathers.

This story shows how ordinary people can play a major part in fighting pollution. All kinds of people thronged to the beaches to pitch in. They worked all night in January weather. What kept them going was the feeling that in fighting for their environment, they were fighting for themselves. The detailed experiences of the San Francisco oil spill have been written down so that the techniques they learned can be used to help other people in the future.

No Happy New Year for the birds!

On New Year's Eve, 1988, wildlife experts were trying to save the lives of 105 seabirds. The birds were found covered with oil on the beaches near Brighton. RSPCA inspectors and volunteers combed a 55 km stretch of the shore.

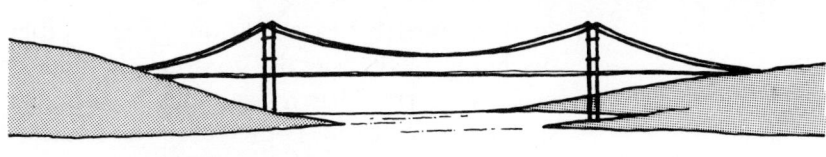

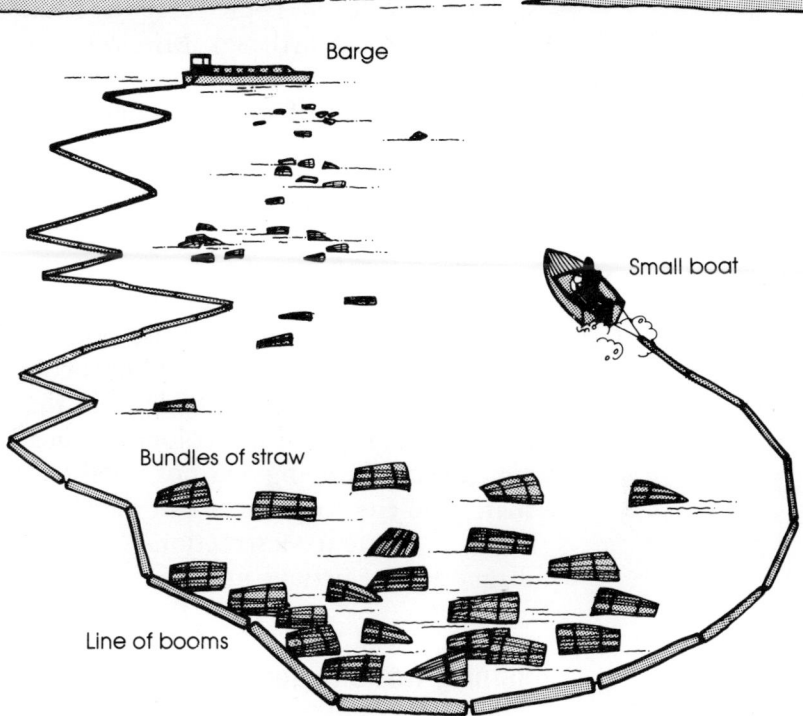

Picking up sodden bales of straw

[Diagram labels: Barge; Small boat; Bundles of straw; Line of booms]

Some birds had to be destroyed. The rest were taken to an RSPCA cleaning centre in Somerset. After some weeks of treatment, many of the birds were returned to the sea.

The Department of Transport began an investigation into the three-mile oil slick washing up on the south coast. A chemist analysed the oil in an attempt to match it with heavy fuel oil from ships known to have passed through the Channel. Investigators concluded that the oil had been washed into the sea by a ship cleaning out its storage tanks. If it had been an accident, it would have been reported. They were unable to identify the ship.

THE NORTH SEA

In the summer of 1988, on the North Sea shores of West Germany, many bathing beaches were covered in a foam of algae. On the island of Sylt, people formed a 40 km long chain — nearly the length of the whole island. The human chain drew attention to the metre-thick blanket of foul-smelling foam that covered the beaches of the resort. The cause was the phosphates and nitrates washing into the North Sea from the agriculture and industry of Europe. The West German Environment Minister proposed spending £6 billion

73

to fight North Sea pollution. Rivers, pipelines and dumpships discharge heavy metals, noxious chemicals and radioactive waste into the North Sea. This load mixes with a tide of sewage. The Rhine is probably the foulest river in Europe. It flows into the North Sea. Britain has the worst record for sewage disposal. Every year, 35 million tonnes of sewage and 9 million tonnes of sewage sludge go into the sea.

There is gathering pressure to clean up the North Sea. West Germany and Belgium are building treatment-plants for industrial waste. In 1987, the Prince of Wales addressed a conference on North Sea pollution. The Prince said, 'Over the last century we have made the North Sea into a rubbish dump. It is really simply no use pointing national fingers at each other in some sort of ugliness contest to find the dirtiest man in Europe.' Prince Charles said that the excuse that there is not enough proof of ecological damage to justify stricter controls on dumping was not good enough. He pointed out that, 'The environment is full of uncertainty. It makes no sense to test it to destruction. While we wait for the doctor's diagnosis, the patient may die.'

Burning waste at sea

Greenpeace is an organisation which works to protect the environment. They have campaigned to stop the burning of waste at sea. In one incident in 1987, a young Briton called Heather Holve boarded a West German incinerator ship, *Vesta*, and handcuffed herself to railings near the furnace of the ship. The ship was burning toxic waste in a zone 100 miles to the east of Scarborough. Heather was prepared to brave the force 10 gale which was forecast, but Dutch police cut her free and arrested her for trespass. The next day, she was back on the Greenpeace ship, *Sirius*, trying to intercept *Vulcanus II*, the biggest incinerator ship in the world. The Dutch-owned *Vulcanus II* had sailed to the North Sea from Spain. The Spanish Government had refused to allow it to burn its cargo of waste off the Spanish coast. The *Vulcanus II* was preparing to burn 2000 tonnes of highly toxic chemical waste off the Yorkshire coast. Heather and other Greenpeace workers tried to board the ship from an inflatable dinghy. The crew of the *Vulcanus II* doused the campaigners with water from high-powered hoses. After several hours, tired and bruised, the Greenpeace party had to admit defeat.

The companies which carry out the burning of wastes at sea say that they dispose of dangerous wastes safely and cheaply. They do not cleanse some of the gases they emit. These are supposed to be absorbed harmlessly into the sea. The idea is that the sea's capacity frees these ships from the need to clean the gases they emit. This is what makes burning waste at sea a cheap method of disposal. In 1985, the Royal Commission on Environmental Pollution supported burning at sea, provided that it was properly policed. It is, of course, very difficult to monitor ships at sea. This is a powerful argument against burning waste at sea. The UK has not only its own wastes to dispose of; we also import waste from other countries to burn and to bury in landfill sites. This service earns the UK some extra income. The National Union of Seamen has joined Greenpeace in calling for a ban on the import of hazardous waste. A problem is that some of the wastes that come here are very dangerous, and the less travelling they do the better. There have been few accidents on our seas involving hazardous wastes. Nevertheless it would be less risky to dispose of such wastes near the plants which created them.

QUESTIONS ON POLLUTION AT SEA

1 (a) What is 'ecological damage'?
(b) What is 'testing to destruction'?
(c) Why does the Prince of Wales think that we should not wait for further proof of damage to the North Sea before we take action on dumping?
(d) What does Prince Charles mean by 'pointing national fingers at each other'? Why is he impatient with this attitude?

2 What is the connection between algae and phosphates (see p. 54–8)? Why are algae found more often in lakes than in the sea?

3 Disposing of waste from other countries earns money for the UK. Why do some people disagree with the practice?

4 What is the advantage of burning waste at sea, instead of on land? Why do some people disagree with burning waste at sea?

5 Methods of disposing of toxic waste include burning on land, burning at sea, burying on land and dumping at sea. State one disadvantage of each method.

6 Some people think that Greenpeace campaigners are heroes; other people think they are freaks. What is your opinion? Explain your answer.

| CASE HISTORY 9 | **The biggest oil spill — the *Exxon Valdez***

The trans-Alaska pipeline carries oil from oil wells in the north of Alaska to the port of Valdez. Tankers fill up with oil at Valdez and then sail south to supply the rest of the USA with oil. On 24 March, 1989, a supertanker called the *Exxon Valdez* left Valdez carrying 350 million litres of oil. Only 40 km out of port, the ship struck a submerged reef, Bligh Reef, which punctured some of the ship's oil tanks. From the holed supertanker leaked 60 million litres of oil. The spill formed an oil slick of 1300 square kilometres in a shallow area called Prince William Sound.

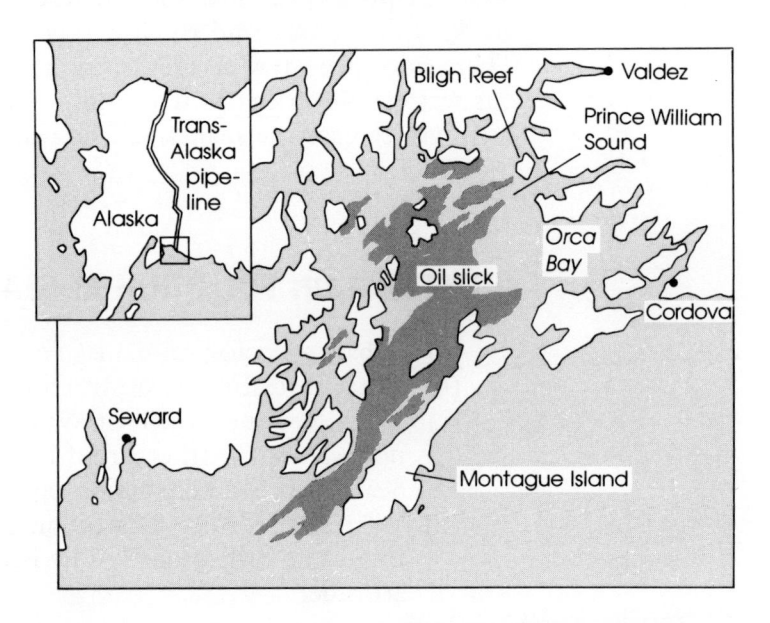

Map of Alaska

A thousand rivers and streams flow into Prince William Sound. The shoreline takes in countless inlets and islands. A huge variety of sea-life from shrimps to whales live in the Sound. Migrating birds stop off there on their route home from wintering in the south. The Sound was one of the unspoilt areas of the world — until 60 million litres of crude oil brought death to the bay.

The ship is owned by Exxon Shipping. After 10 hours the company tried to stop the spill spreading. By that time, high winds and choppy seas had made it difficult to apply any of the methods of dealing with spills. For five days, Exxon Shipping did little to minimise the effects of the spill. Failure to contain the spill allowed it to move out of Prince William Sound and reach the shoreline. Exxon Shipping and Alyeska, the company which operates the oil terminal at Valdez, recruited 600 people to clean up the mess. Their first efforts were to try to prevent the oil spreading further and to rescue birds and sea-mammals caught in the slick. Scientists from a number of organisations travelled to the area to give help and advice.

Scientists expect that the rocky parts of the coastline will soon be cleansed by the action of waves breaking against them. Other shores are lined with a coarse gravel into which oil can sink. The oil could remain there for 3–10 years. Exxon Shipping scrubbed 560 km of oil-soaked coastline clean during the summer of 1989. Workers blasted rock faces with hot water under high pressure, and washed sand and gravel with cold water under low pressure.

Exxon Shipping suspended its clean-up operation in September, 1989, annoying the Alaskan authorities. The state of Alaska must finance their own winter clean-up, spending some $21 million.

The effects on marine life

Sea-mammals

Thousands of sea-mammals live in the polluted area of Prince William Sound. Sea lions, seals and sea otters have suffered from the pollution. One expert thinks that the smell of some of the compounds in crude oil may have actually drawn sea-mammals to the slick. Sea otters that become covered with oil have no chance of recovering without human assistance. Unlike other marine animals, sea otters do not have an insulating layer of fat. They keep warm by means of a coat of short dense fur. This is protected by an outer layer of long guard hairs. If the guard hairs become soiled, the fur underneath becomes wet. Then the fur can no longer keep the animal warm and it can no longer trap air and keep the animal buoyant. As a result, the otter drowns. Many sea-mammals can escape by swimming away from polluted areas.

Sea otters

Sea otters are very much at risk because they do not swim well over long distances, so they cannot escape from the polluted area. In addition, they need to eat a large weight of fish every day, so they suffer when the fish are poisoned.

Exxon Shipping and the US Government set up a rescue operation. A fleet of 30 fishing boats and a staff of 200 people rescued sea otters and took them to 10 cleaning stations. There are about 10 000 sea otters in Prince William Sound. Of the sea otters which have been rescued and cleaned, only half have survived. Post-mortems have shown that the otters were poisoned by oil. A vet reported that in two post-mortems he had done the livers of sea otters had 'gone through his fingers like paste'. A wide range of disorders of liver, brain, heart and central nervous system have been found in marine mammals living in the area of the spill.

By mid-September, 1989, 10 000 sea otters and 16 whales had died.

Birds

Every year in May, 15 million migrating birds arrive in Alaska. Only 100 km from Prince William Sound is the world's largest stop-over for migrating birds, the Copper River delta. Waders stop in the shallow water there, 11 million of them, on their way home from wintering in the south. Some of them come from as far away as Panama. Oil could affect waders in two ways: they could swallow the oil or the oil could kill off their food.

The fouled shorelines all along Prince William Sound are important habitats for birds. We do not know yet how these birds will be affected.

Seabirds began to arrive while the oil spill clogged the open water where they feed on fish and plankton. Seabirds spend the summer in Prince William Sound. The US Fish and Wildlife Service began, early in May 1989, to use rockets, crackers and assorted fireworks to try to scare birds away from the contaminated areas. The length of polluted coastline is so great that the Service says 'You would need a large army to protect all the birds.'

By mid-September, 1989, 34 434 seabirds and 147 bald eagles had died.

Fish

Some of the compounds in crude oil affect the nervous systems of fish, making them drowsy so that they do not escape from predators.

METHODS OF DEALING WITH OIL SLICKS

Over the years, experience of dealing with oil slicks has led to the development of a number of techniques. None of them is very reliable. The problem remains a difficult and dangerous one.

Dispersants

Chemical dispersants can be used to break down the slick. They are now more effective and less toxic than those used during the *Torrey Canyon* disaster. The dispersants break up the oil into small droplets which are dispersed and diluted by the ocean. Exxon Shipping was too late: by the time they applied dispersants in Alaska, the sea had churned up the oil slick into an emulsion. This 'chocolate mousse', as one worker described it, reacted very slowly with the dispersants.

Skimming oil off the sea

Booms are large fireproof tubes. A boat can place a line of booms round an oil slick (see the diagram on p. 73 to stop the oil spreading. Then skimmers can get to work scooping oil off the surface. This is not easy in a rough sea. In a current of only one kilometre per hour oil can seep under the booms. High winds and waves lift the oil over the boom. Most of the oil slick in Alaska escaped from the booms which were placed around it.

Burning

Sometimes the oil slick can be burnt off the water. Weather conditions must be right for the oil to burn safely. The sea must be calm and the wind slight, and the oil must not have started to disperse. The technique is to ignite the oil by tossing a 'torch' from a helicopter on to the oil in the slick. Some experts think that Exxon could have burnt off the oil slick if they had tackled it before it spread.

Solidifying the oil

Chemists at the British Petroleum Company have discovered chemicals that have an amazing effect on oil. When sprayed on to a film of oil, they turn it slowly into a dry, rubbery solid. Chunks of the oil can be collected in nets. If any of the solidified oil escapes the nets, and washes ashore, it can be peeled off the beach like a rubber sheet. The chemicals have been tried out in the laboratory and also in experiments at sea. One day, they may prove their worth in fighting pollution.

QUESTIONS ON OIL SPILLS

1 What equipment should an oil terminal have in readiness for dealing with oil spills?

2 At first, people reading about the *Exxon Valdez* accident thought that Alaska was too far away to concern them. How does the pollution affect other parts of the world?

3 What conditions made the Valdez accident a suitable case for trying to burn off the oil? Under what conditions is this method very dangerous?

4 From what you have read, what do you think would have been the best way to tackle the Alaskan spill?

5 Explain why seabirds are killed by oil spills.

6 Explain why sea otters suffer from oil spills. What could happen to a sea otter that was rescued, cleaned and returned to the sea?

7 The table shows gel times for the treatment of Alaskan oil by the method invented by the BP chemists.

Temperature ($°C$)	Gel time (in minutes) when treated with gelling agent		
	10%	7.5%	5.0%
25	3.5	4.0	8.5
20	4.0	5.0	12.5
15	5.0	7.0	20.0
10	7.0	8.0	
5	10.0	13.0	
0	14.5	20.0	

(a) On graph paper, plot gel time against temperature for (i) 10% gelling agent, (ii) 7.5% gelling agent, (iii) 5.0% gelling agent.
(b) The method works well in the laboratory. What is the difficulty in making this method work in the open sea?
(c) Why does the coast of Alaska have difficult conditions for this method to work?

ACTIVITY 12

Ways of cleaning oil-soaked feathers

Step 1 Look at the way the feathers repel water. Drop water on to a feather from a teat pipette. See how the water runs off the surface.

Step 2 Smear sump oil on six feathers.

Step 3 Put a 1 per cent solution of soap flakes into a boiling tube. Put one of the feathers into the boiling tube. Leave it for 5 minutes. Move it gently around from time to time. After 5 minutes, take it out, and leave it to dry.

With the other feathers, try other cleaning agents, e.g. solutions of detergents, and solvents such as propanone and ethanol. *These are flammable liquids. Take care.* You must NOT have a lighted Bunsen or any other flame around.

Step 4 When the feathers are dry, look at them carefully. Make a note of which looks the cleanest. Now test the feathers you have cleaned to see how they repel water. Which treatment has the worst effect on the feathers' ability to repel water?

Extension Work You can try rubbing feathers with cleaning agents and solvents, instead of soaking them. You can try taking off the oil with an absorbent material such as sawdust.

QUESTIONS ON POLLUTION

1. The word *pollution* has been used many times in this book. Explain what is meant by pollution of water. What are the most common causes of pollution in rivers? What are the most common causes of pollution in lakes? Is it possible to pollute the sea?

2. The word *conservation* is used to mean keeping our environment clean and healthy. Explain what needs to be done to keep rivers and lakes clean.

3. List all the recreational uses for rivers and lakes that you can think of. Do any of these uses pollute the water?

4. Recently countries have agreed to stop dumping steel canisters containing waste chemicals into the North Sea.

    Explain (a) how the chemicals could escape from the canisters, (b) how they could be a danger to people.

CROSSWORD ON WATER POLLUTION

First, trace this grid on to a piece of paper (or photocopy this page). Then fill in the answers. Do not write on this page.

Across

2 See 5 across
5, 2 across This mammal suffered in the *Exxon Valdez* accident (3, 5)
6 She sounds like a mixed-up seal (4)
7, 13 across A ___ of ___ is one method of containing an oil spill (4, 5)
8 Part of a fish that can be hard or soft (3)
9 This way of getting rid of an oil slick can be dangerous (4)
11 Many birds have been ___ by oil pollution (6)
12 See 3 down
13 See 7 across
16 Oil can leak ___ 7 across, 13 across in a current (5)
18 Oil will ___ out of a holed 10 down (4)
19 The state where the biggest oil spill happened (6)

Down

1 An oil spill on water (5)
2 Less than two (3)
3, 12 across This 10 down sank in 1967 (6, 6)
4 The cause of the *Exxon Valdez* accident (4)
5 All sea captains should put this first (6)
10 It transports oil (6)
12 This is what Exxon Shipping promised to do to the shores of Alaska (5)
14 Not quite circular (4)
15 One way of removing oil from the sea is to ___ it up (4)
17 This caused the collision in San Francisco Bay (3)

SOME QUESTIONS FOR DISCUSSION

You may like to form a group to tackle these questions.

QUESTION 1
(a) Will we ever get rid of pollution?
(b) How much pollution should we put up with?
(c) Who should pay for cleaning-up polluted water?

QUESTION 2
Imagine that, in order to cure the acute shortage of housing in your area, the council has decided to turn the local park into a site for building a housing estate. The park consists of a large area of natural woodland with a nature trail, a small lake and a large safe adventure playground for children. The council has set up a meeting to allow residents to give their views on the plan. You have been asked to speak at the meeting. You oppose the idea of turning the park into a housing estate. What points will you make in your speech to convince people of the importance of retaining the park? (If, on the other hand, you agree with sacrificing the park for a new housing estate, you should put forward your reasons.)

A FINAL WORD: POLLUTION AND CONSERVATION

What is water?

Water is a compound of hydrogen and oxygen. It has the formula H_2O. It is a very good solvent for many substances.

What is pure water?

Pure water is water which contains no dissolved substances. It is very difficult to obtain pure water as it is such a good solvent for many substances. It tends to dissolve a little of any substance with which it comes into contact. Distillation can be used to give pure water.

What is polluted water?

We call water 'polluted' when it contains substances which are harmful to life. A polluted river has less plant life and fewer fish than a clean river. The main sources of pollution are:
1) People's body waste — sewage
2) Industrial waste
3) Insecticides and fertilisers.

Why do we need to protect water from pollution?

Diseases are spread by dirty water. Polluted water is a danger to health.

Polluted water is likely to become unpleasant and smelly. People like to use rivers and lakes for recreation. They cannot enjoy themselves in polluted water.

River-water is taken to the water-treatment works and made fit to drink. If the river-water is polluted, the treatment is much more costly. It may even become impossible to make the water fit to drink.

What is conservation?

The word conservation means keeping things the same. People talk about *conservation of the environment*. By *environment*, they mean the world about us — the air, the water and the land. By *conservation* of the environment, they mean keeping the air, water and the land in the same clean and healthy state it was in before our society became so industrialised. People who are very interested in conservation are called *conservationists*. Conservationists are not opposed to progress. They do not want to do without the benefits of modern industry. What they do want is for us to keep a sharp lookout for the side-effects of industry. Some of these side-effects are polluting the air, the water and the land. Conservationists want us to make sure that our lives do not become poorer because we have let our environment become unhealthy and unclean.

Have you ever thought about doing your bit towards conservation? You may not be in a position to do what the people of San Francisco did, but there is plenty you can do. You could get a group together and go round with sacks, picking up litter. You will be surprised how much you enjoy it if there is a group of you working together. You could reclaim a spoiled area. Some girls we know saw an area near their school that was an eyesore. They weeded it, sowed some grass seed and planted some shrubs and flowers. Now it is a very eye-catching corner. It gives them satisfaction to see it on their way to school, and know that it is all due to them. Some boys and girls we know worked on the banks of a canal. They weeded, and removed dead wood and litter. They uncovered a footpath which had become overgrown. People can now walk along the canal. It is now a pleasant area for recreation. The group who did the conservation work enjoy it more than anyone.

HOW DO YOUR RESULTS COMPARE WITH OURS?

Activity 2, p. 19

1) (a) about 1 litre or 2 pints (b) 4 to 9 litres or 1 to 2 gallons (c) varies, about 4 to 9 litres, 1 to 2 gallons (d) 45 litres or 10 gallons (e) 4 to 9 litres or 1 to 2 gallons.
2) (a) 5 litres or 1.1 gallons (b) 50 litres or 10 gallons (c) 15 litres or 3.3 gallons (d) 50 litres or 10 gallons (e) 15 litres or 3.3 gallons (f) 15 litres or 3.3 gallons.

Activity 8, p. 36

Distillation gives the softest water. It is too expensive for use in the home. Permutit® gives the next best result, and is suitable for use in the home. Washing soda is cheap and is a good water-softener.

Activity 10, p. 37

Experiment 1 Step 1 Powder is not dispersed at all.
Step 2(1) Powder disperses at first, but soon sinks to the bottom or rises with scum. 2(2) A good permanent dispersion. 2(3) The result depends on the relative amounts of soap and detergent in the brand used.
Experiment 2 The layer of oil is thinner in the test-tube (2) with detergent added. Detergent makes oil mix with water: detergents are emulsifying agents.
Experiment 3 (1), (3) and (4) lather; (2) has scum. Detergent lathers in hard water but soap does not.
Experiment 4 Examples are Stergene® pH 7 to 8, Lux® flakes 10 to 11, washing-machine detergent 10 to 11, washing-up liquids 7 to 8.
Experiment 5 Enzyme detergent works better, especially on food stains.

ANSWERS TO SELECTED QUESTIONS

Chapter 1

p. 16   (b) They can obtain less oxygen.
        (c) The body temperature of the fish drops.

p. 23   5   (b) 476 litres   (c) 88.2 litres

Chapter 3

p. 44   6   (b) (i) 29%   (ii) 45%

Chapter 4

p. 61 2 (b) (i) 2.0 tonne/hectare (ii) 1.5 tonne/hectare
           (iii) 0.3 tonne/hectare

p. 62 1 (c) not more than 20 kg/hectare

p. 66 2 (a) (i) 8.15 (ii) 7.3
           (c) (i) 10.24 mg/litre (ii) 10.68 mg/litre
               (iii) Difference = 0.44 mg/litre = 4.1%
           (d) (i) 3.9 mg/litre (ii) 2.4 mg/litre
               (iii) Difference = 1.5 mg/litre = 38%
           (f) (i) 9.585 mg/litre (ii) 2.68 mg/litre
               (iii) Difference = 6.91 mg/litre

p. 67 3 (a) Medway (b) improved
           (c) first worsened; then improved

INDEX

Agriculture 54–61
Air 12
Alaska 76–8
Algae 56, 57
Aluminium 17
Amoco Cadiz 69
Animal life 15, 19
Aswan Dam 25

Bacteria 5, 7, 53
Bilharzia 27
Biochemical oxygen demand, BOD 15
Burning waste 74

Cesspit 2, 4
Chlorine 3, 4
Conservation 84
Copper 16
Cornish water 17
Crosswords 24, 31, 45, 82

Detergents 34–5, 37–44
Dibden filter 7
Diseases 2, 5
Drinking-water 2–4, 9, 59–60

Egypt 25
Enzyme detergents 40, 43
Estuaries 51
European Community, EC 59, 61
Eutrophication 55–7
Exxon Valdez 76

Fertilisers 54–7
Fish 78
Fluoride 9–11

Germs 5
Greenpeace 74
Ground-water 58

Hard water 34
Herbicides 61

Insecticides 61

Lake Erie 55
Lake Nasser 25–8
Landfill 75
Lather 34
Lead pipes 64
Lime 7
Lough Neagh 57

Mercury 52
Methane 12
Micro-organisms 5, 7, 49, 53

Minamata 52
Model water-purifier 21
Model water-softener 36

National Rivers Authority 48
Nitrate 54–60
Norfolk Broads 57
North Sea 73

Oil 68, 79–80
  burning 79
  dispersants 79
  skimming 79
  solidifying 79
Osmosis 28
Oxidation of sewage 7, 11, 15
Oxygen 8, 11, 14–16, 56

Pesticides 61
Plants 28
Prince Charles 74
Privatisation 64

Reservoir 3
River Irwell 46
River Nile 25
River Rhine 49
River Thames 4
Rivers 46

Safe water 12, 14
Salmon 4, 8
Salt 26
San Francisco 71
Sandoz 50
Scum 34
Seabirds 70, 78
Sea-mammals 77
Sea otters 77
Sewage 4–7, 53–4
Sewage-works 11-13, 18, 53–4
Sewers 5
Silt 6, 26
Sludge ship 13
Soap 32, 35, 37
Soft water 34

Thermal pollution 15
Torrey Canyon 69
Transpiration 13, 28
Treatment of water 4–8, 11–12

Uses for water 1, 19, 21

Water authorities and companies 48–60
Water-closet 5
Water cycle 14
Wordfinder 18

87